GCSE
Success

English
Language & Literature

Paul Burns

Practice Test Papers

Contents

Acknowledgements

The author and publisher are grateful to the copyright holders for permission to use quoted materials and images.

P.31, 50, 74 'The War of the Worlds' by H G Wells. Used with permission of The Literary Executors of the Estate of H G Wells; P.35, 54 'Hobson's Choice' by Harold Brighouse, published by Samuel French Ltd. Reprinted by permission of Samuel French Ltd; P.35, 54 'Journey's End' by R.C. Sherriff. Reproduced by permission of Curtis Brown Group Ltd; P.35, 55, 76 *The Woman in Black* by Susan Hill, published by Vintage Books © Susan Hill 1983. Reproduced by permission of Sheil Land Associates Ltd; P.36, 55 Oranges are Not the Only Fruit by Jeanette Winterson, reprinted by permission of Peters Fraser & Dunlop (www.petersfraserdunlop.com) on behalf of Jeanette Winterson; P.51 'An Inspector Calls' by J.B. Priestley (Heinemann, 1945). Reproduced by permission of Penguin Books Ltd; P.51, 83 'Blood Brothers' © Willy Russell, 2001, 'Blood Brothers'. Reprinted by permission of Bloomsbury Methuen Drama, an imprint of Bloomsbury Publishing Plc; P.52, 83 'The History Boys' by Alan Bennett. Used with permission of Faber and Faber Publishing; P.52, 75, 84 © Simon Stephens, 2004, *The Curious Incident of the Dog in the Night-Time*. Reprinted by permission of Bloomsbury Methuen Drama, an imprint of Bloomsbury Publishing Plc; P.52, 84

'A Taste of Honey' © Shelagh Delaney, revised edition 2008, 'A Taste of Honey', Bloomsbury Methuen Drama, an imprint of Bloomsbury Publishing Plc. And with kind permission of Sayle Screen; P.53 'Lord of the Flies' by William Golding. Used with permission of Faber and Faber Publishing; *P.53, 84 Animal Farm* by George Orwell (Copyright © George Orwell, 1945) Reprinted by permission of Bill Hamilton as the Literary Executor of the Estate of the Late Sonia Brownell Orwell; P.53 'Never Let Me Go' by Kazuo Ishiguro. Used with permission of Faber and Faber Publishing; P.54 'Anita and Me' by Meera Syal. Used with permission of Rogers, Coleridge and White; P.55 'My Mother Said I Never Should' © Charlotte Keatley, 1988, 'My Mother Said I Never Should', Bloomsbury Methuen Drama, an imprint of Bloomsbury Publishing Plc.

Images are © Shutterstock.com

Every effort has been made to trace copyright holders and obtain their permission for the use of copyright material. The author and publisher will gladly receive information enabling them to rectify any error or omission in subsequent editions. All facts are correct at time of going to press.

Published by Letts Educational
An imprint of HarperCollins*Publishers*
1 London Bridge Street
London SE1 9GF

ISBN: 978-0-00-816967-1

First published 2016

10 9 8 7 6 5 4 3 2

© HarperCollins*Publishers* Limited

British Library Cataloguing in Publication Data.

A CIP record of this book is available from the British Library.

Commissioning Editor: Emily Linnett
Author: Paul Burns
Project Management and Editorial: Katie Galloway
Cover Design: Sarah Duxbury and Paul Oates
Inside Concept Design: Paul Oates
Production: Lyndsey Rogers
Text Design and Layout: Contentra Technologies
Printed in China by RR Donnelley APS

English Language Practice Papers Set A

Pages 4–7: English Language Paper 1: Reading Literary Texts and Creative Writing

The questions on pages 4–7 will help you to revise for:

- AQA Paper 1: Explorations in Creative Reading and Writing
- Edexcel Paper 1: Fiction and Imaginative Writing
- OCR Paper 2: Exploring Effects and Impact
- WJEC Eduqas Component 1: 20th Century Literature Reading and Creative Prose Writing

The marks for the questions are shown in brackets.

There are 40 marks for Section A (reading) and 40 marks for Section B (writing). The maximum mark for this paper is 80.

Pages 8–12: English Language Paper 2: Reading Non-fiction and Non-fiction/Transactional Writing

The questions on pages 8–12 will help you to revise for:

- AQA Paper 2: Writers' Viewpoints and Perspectives
- Edexcel Paper 2: Non-fiction and Transactional Writing
- OCR Paper 1: Communicating Information and Ideas
- WJEC Eduqas Component 2: 19th and 20th Century Non-fiction Reading and Transactional/Persuasive Writing

The marks for the questions are shown in brackets.

There are 40 marks for Section A (reading) and 40 marks for Section B (writing). The maximum mark for this paper is 80.

Name: _____

English Language Paper 1: Reading Literary Texts and Creative Writing

Section A: Reading

You are advised to spend one hour on this section: about 10 minutes reading, about 50 minutes answering the questions.

Read carefully the passage below. Then answer all the questions in this section.

This extract is the opening of 'Home Sickness', a short story by George Moore, first published in 1903. The story opens in New York.

He told the doctor he was due in the bar-room at eight o'clock in the morning; the bar-room was in a slum in the Bowery; and he had only been able to keep himself in health by getting up at five o'clock and going for long walks in the Central Park.

"A sea voyage is what you want," said the doctor. "Why not go to Ireland for two or three
5 months? You will come back a new man."

"I'd like to see Ireland again."

And he began to wonder how the people at home were getting on. The doctor was right. He thanked him, and three weeks afterwards he landed in Cork.

As he sat in the railway carriage he recalled his native village, built among the rocks of the
10 large headland stretching out into the winding lake. He could see the houses and the streets, and the fields of the tenants, and the Georgian mansion and the owners of it; he and they had been boys together before he went to America. He remembered the villagers going every morning to the big house to work in the stables, in the garden, in the fields - mowing, reaping, digging, and Michael Malia building a wall; it was all as clear as if it were yesterday, yet he had been thirteen
15 years in America; and when the train stopped at the station, the first thing he did was to look round for any changes that might have come into it. It was the same blue limestone station as it was thirteen years ago, with the same five long miles between it and Duncannon. He had once walked these miles gaily, in a little over an hour, carrying a heavy bundle on a stick, but he did not feel strong enough for the walk today, though the evening tempted him to try it. A car[1] was
20 waiting at the station, and the boy, discerning from his accent and his dress that Bryden had come from America, plied him with questions, which Bryden answered rapidly, for he wanted to hear who were still living in the village, and if there was a house in which he could get a clean lodging. The best house in the village, he was told, was Mike Scully's, who had been away in a situation for many years, as a coachman in the King's County, but had come back and built a fine house with a
25 concrete floor. The boy could recommend the loft, he had slept in it himself, and Mike would be glad to take in a lodger, he had no doubt. Bryden remembered that Mike had been in a situation at the Big House. He had intended to be a jockey, but had suddenly shot up into a fine tall man, and had had to become a coachman instead; and Bryden tried to recall the face, but he could only remember a straight nose, and a somewhat dusky complexion.

30   So Mike had come back from King's County, and had built himself a house, had married –
there were children for sure running about; while he, Bryden, had gone to America, but he had
come back; perhaps he, too, would build a house in Duncannon, and – his reverie was suddenly
interrupted by the carman.

        'There's Mike Scully,' he said, pointing with his whip, and Bryden saw a tall, finely-built,
35 middle-aged man coming through the gates, who looked astonished when he was accosted, for he
had forgotten Bryden even more completely than Bryden had forgotten him; and many aunts and
uncles were mentioned before he began to understand.

        'You've grown into a fine man, James,' he said, looking at Bryden's great width of chest. 'But
you're thin in the cheeks, and you're very sallow in the cheeks too.'

40   'I haven't been well lately - that is one of the reasons I've come back; but I want to see you all
again.'

        'And thousand welcome you are.'

¹*car – here a cab, drawn by a horse, for hire like a taxi*

1.   Pick two phrases from lines 1–9 that tell us that Bryden is originally from Ireland.

....

.... **[2 marks]**

2.   **a)** What is the name of the village that Bryden came from?

.... **[1 mark]**

     b) How far is the village from the railway station?

.... **[1 mark]**

3.   Look at lines 1 to 8 (*from* 'He told the doctor…' *to* '…he landed in Cork.')

     This extract is the beginning of a short story.

     How does the writer make the reader interested in what might happen next?

     You could write about:
     • what happens to build the reader's interest
     • how the writer uses language and structure to interest the reader.   **[8 marks]**

4. Read lines 9 to 16 (*from* 'As he sat...' *to* '...any changes that might have come into it.')

How does the writer use language to create an impression of life in Duncannon?

You could include the writer's choice of:
- words and phrases
- language features and techniques
- sentence forms.

[8 marks]

5. 'In James Bryden, the writer has created a protagonist that readers can sympathise with. We really want to know the outcome of his return to Ireland.'

How far do you agree with this statement?

- Write about your own impressions of James Bryden and his return to Ireland.
- Evaluate how the writer has created these impressions.
- Support your opinions with quotations from the text.

[20 marks]

Section B: Writing

You are advised to spend 45 minutes on this section: about 10 minutes planning, about 35 minutes writing.

6. **EITHER**

    a) Write a description suggested by this picture.

    OR

    b) Write a story that begins 'I sat on the park bench and thought about what the doctor had said.'

    [24 marks for content and organisation and 16 marks for technical accuracy; total 40 marks]

END OF QUESTIONS

English Language Paper 2: Reading
Non-fiction and Non-fiction/Transactional Writing

Section A: Reading

Answer all questions in this section.

You are advised to spend 45 minutes on this section.

Source A is an extract from *The Food of London*, by George Dodd, published in 1856. In this chapter the writer describes how bread is made in London and compares it to what is happening in Paris and Birmingham.

The bread-making processes are, indeed, clumsily managed in the majority of London establishments. Whoever has seen the rude and primitive mode in which dough is kneaded, by a man straddling and wriggling on the end of a lever or pole, may well marvel that such uncouthness should not long ago have been superseded by something better. Our Parisian neighbours appear to be somewhat in the same plight as
5 ourselves. On a recent occasion, M. Payen, a distinguished French chemist, made a Report to the Academie Française on the bread and baking of Paris. He said: "A day will doubtless come when our descendants, who shall read the technology of the 19th century, will ask themselves whether at this time of industrial progress we really prepared the chief of our aliments by the rude way which we now witness – in plunging the arms into the dough, lifting it up and crushing it down with such effort as to exhaust the energy of the half-naked
10 arms, and make the perspiration run down into the food; whether at such an epoch the baking was effected on the very hearth itself from whence the fuel had just been withdrawn; whether it could be believed that during these fatiguing operations the chief part of the heat should seem destined to heat, or rather to roast, the workmen, than to bake the bread!" The Parisian practice is tolerably well marked out in this passage; but improvements seem to be in progress. A committee of the Academie, MM. Payen, Poncelet, and Boussingault,
15 have reported in high terms on a system invented and patented by M. Rolland, in which a kneading machine, worked by hand, will knead a sack of flour into dough in 20 minutes, with a vast saving of muscular labour.

It is strange that, in the greatest city in the world, we have nothing that can be called a large bread-factory. Steam-mills there are on a gigantic scale, as has already been noticed; biscuit-bakeries, in which steam-power is employed to mix and knead the dough; bakers who make frequent changes and
20 improvements in their ovens; but no establishment wherein the plain familiar four pound loaf is made by machinery.

[…] There are now six large bread mills in Birmingham … At one of the largest of these mills, belonging to Mr Lucy, lately Mayor of Birmingham, steam-worked cranes haul up the sacks of wheat from a canal of granaries at the top of the building; steam works fourteen pairs of millstones to grind
25 the corn; steam mixes the wheat before grinding, and the flour after grinding; steam kneads the flour, and water, and yeast, and salt into well-made dough; and then comes the manipulative processes. The bakehouse has tables of large size, and around its walls are eight ovens of great capacity. The dough is made into loaves; the loaves are nicely baked in the ovens; and the baked bread is placed on shelves in a storeroom which will contain 2000 loaves. The mill sells flour as well as bread. At an early hour in the
30 mornings waggons draw up to the mill; they are filled with loaves, which are quickly conveyed to the several hucksters' shops[1], and the waggoner, or attendant servant, returns with the ready money. The huckster sells the bread to the families of the working men of Birmingham.

[1]*Hucksters' shops — shops that sell a variety of goods cheaply*

Source B is an advertising feature for a local bakery.

Archie's Artisan Bakery

Welcome!

Here at Archie's Artisan Bakery, we're putting baking back into the heart of the community. Step into our village bakery and you'll be greeted by the smell of freshly baked bread - a smell that says 'home' - and the sight of a dazzling array of breads,
5 *pastries and cakes.*

Archie and Fab

Hi, I'm Archie Bold, the co-owner of Archie's Artisan Bakery, and the master baker. I'm a local lad, coming from a long line of bakers and confectioners. After attending a local catering
10 college and spending a year as a sous chef at a Michelin starred London restaurant, I felt the family trade calling. But I was also aware of how many of the traditional skills have been lost here in Britain. To get the best possible training, I took myself off to France, where I trained with some of the world's best artisan
15 bakers.

I also fell in love, not just with French baking but with *maîtresse patissiere*, 'Fab' Fabienne Rollard. Five years later we're married and I've fulfilled my childhood dream by opening my own bakery in the beautiful village of Rotterthwaite, just ten miles from my hometown.

20 Today, Fab's fabulous choux pastry creations bring a touch of Parisian sophistication to our village bakery, sitting happily alongside more traditional British cakes, many inspired by old family recipes.

Real Bread!

25 What do we mean by real bread? Well, we don't mean white sliced pre-packaged bread, full of additives and made on an industrial scale in huge factories. Nor do we mean the bread that you might find in your local supermarket, supposedly 'baked on the premises' when in fact it has been half-baked somewhere else, driven miles in a van to your local store and then 'finished off' quickly.

Real bread - or artisan bread as it's often called - is made with just four things: flour, water, salt
30 and yeast.

In France a shop can only call itself a *boulangerie* if all five processes involved in bread making - fermentation, mixing, kneading, shaping and baking - happen in the one place. We don't have that rule in Britain, but that's exactly what happens at Archie's. And it's all done by hand.

I believe that real bread is more than food for the body - it's food for the soul. My assistants, Stan
35 and Rita, and I bring years of experience and expertise to our craft. We also bring passion and love. A real baker bakes not just with the head and the hands, but with the heart.

How We Make Our Bread

For us, local ingredients are key. We source our ingredients locally wherever possible. Our top
40 quality organic flour, for example, comes from Gorton's Mills just thirty miles down the road. The bread making process starts with 'starter', created from flour and water and natural yeast - wild yeasts for our increasingly popular
45 sourdough range.

A good loaf takes many hours to create. And a good baker needs patience as well as skill and flair.

After we've shaped our loaves and allowed them to gently rise, they are baked in our
50 traditional oven.

In this way we can produce over 200 top quality loaves of the finest artisan breads each day - sourdoughs, baguettes, wholemeal, crusty white, granary and even gluten-free.

Visit Us!

We are open from Monday to Saturday between 8.30 a.m. and 5.00 p.m. and you're welcome to
55 visit and see us at work whenever the shop is open. We'll even show you round the bakery and share some of our secrets.

We also have a local delivery service and you can order your bread and cakes the day before you want them, either online, by telephone or just by popping into the shop. Keep in touch with us via our website where you'll find full details (and mouth-watering pictures!) of all our delicious products.

1. Read again Source A from lines 1 to 16.

Choose four statements below which are TRUE.
- Shade the boxes of the ones that you think are true.
- Choose a maximum of four statements.

A. Bakers in London and Paris make bread in a similar way. ☐

B. M. Payen is a biologist. ☐

C. The writer thinks all bread should be made by hand. ☐

D. M. Rolland has invented a machine for kneading dough. ☐

E. M. Payen has written a novel about bakers in Paris. ☐

F. Most of the heat from the Paris bread ovens is wasted. ☐

G. Making bread is physically hard work. ☐

H. The committee of the Academie Française was not impressed by Rolland's system. ☐

[4 marks]

2. You need to refer to Source A and Source B for this question.

Use details from both sources. Write a summary of the differences between Lucy's bread mill and Archie's Artisan Bakery. **[8 marks]**

3. You now need to refer only to Source B, the advertising feature for Archie's Artisan Bakery.

How does the writer use language to try to engage and influence the reader? **[12 marks]**

4. For this question you need to refer to both Source A and Source B.

Compare how the writers convey different attitudes to bread-making.

In your answer you should:
- Compare the different attitudes.
- Compare the methods they use to convey these attitudes.
- Support your ideas with quotations from both texts. **[16 marks]**

Section B: Writing

You are advised to spend 45 minutes on this section.

You are reminded of the need to plan your answer.

You should write in full sentences.

You should leave enough time to check your work at the end.

5. 'It's all very well for celebrity TV chefs to go on about healthy eating and not buying convenience food, but when you're working hard and managing on a budget, you simply haven't got the time or energy to follow their advice.'

Write an article for a broadsheet newspaper in which you explain your point of view on this statement.

[24 marks for content and organisation and 16 marks for technical accuracy; total 40 marks]

END OF QUESTIONS

English Language Practice Papers Set B

**Pages 14–17: English Language Paper 1: Reading Literary Texts
and Creative Writing**

The questions on pages 14–17 will help you to revise for:

- AQA Paper 1: Explorations in Creative Reading and Writing
- Edexcel Paper 1: Fiction and Imaginative Writing
- OCR Paper 2: Exploring Effects and Impact
- WJEC Eduqas Component 1: 20th Century Literature Reading and Creative Prose Writing

The marks for the questions are shown in brackets.

There are 40 marks for Section A (reading) and 40 marks for Section B (writing). The maximum mark for this paper is 80.

**Pages 18–22: English Language Paper 2: Reading Non-fiction and
Non-fiction/Transactional Writing**

The questions on pages 18–22 will help you to revise for:

- AQA Paper 2: Writers' Viewpoints and Perspectives
- Edexcel Paper 2: Non-fiction and Transactional Writing
- OCR Paper 1: Communicating Information and Ideas
- WJEC Eduqas Component 2: 19th and 20th Century Non-fiction Reading and Transactional/Persuasive Writing

The marks for the questions are shown in brackets.

There are 40 marks for Section A (reading) and 40 marks for Section B (writing). The maximum mark for this paper is 80.

Name: ....

English Language Paper 1:
Reading Literary Texts and Creative Writing

Section A: Reading

You are advised to spend one hour on this section: about 10 minutes reading, about 50 minutes answering the questions.

Read carefully the passage below. Then answer all the questions in this section.

This text is a complete short story, 'The Story of an Hour', by Kate Chopin, first published in 1894.

> Knowing that Mrs. Mallard was afflicted with a heart trouble, great care was taken to break to her as gently as possible the news of her husband's death.
>
> It was her sister Josephine who told her, in broken sentences; veiled hints that revealed in half concealing. Her husband's friend Richards was there, too, near her. It was he who had been in the
> 5 newspaper office when intelligence of the railroad disaster was received, with Brently Mallard's name leading the list of "killed." He had only taken the time to assure himself of its truth by a second telegram, and had hastened to forestall any less careful, less tender friend in bearing the sad message.
>
> She did not hear the story as many women have heard the same, with a paralyzed inability to accept its significance. She wept at once, with sudden, wild abandonment, in her sister's arms. When
> 10 the storm of grief had spent itself she went away to her room alone. She would have no one follow her.
>
> There stood, facing the open window, a comfortable, roomy armchair. Into this she sank, pressed down by a physical exhaustion that haunted her body and seemed to reach into her soul.
>
> She could see in the open square before her house the tops of trees that were all aquiver with the new spring life. The delicious breath of rain was in the air. In the street below a peddler was
> 15 crying his wares. The notes of a distant song which some one was singing reached her faintly, and countless sparrows were twittering in the eaves.
>
> There were patches of blue sky showing here and there through the clouds that had met and piled one above the other in the west facing her window.
>
> She sat with her head thrown back upon the cushion of the chair, quite motionless, except when
> 20 a sob came up into her throat and shook her, as a child who has cried itself to sleep continues to sob in its dreams.
>
> She was young, with a fair, calm face, whose lines bespoke repression and even a certain strength. But now there was a dull stare in her eyes, whose gaze was fixed away off yonder on one of those patches of blue sky. It was not a glance of reflection, but rather indicated a suspension of
> 25 intelligent thought.
>
> There was something coming to her and she was waiting for it, fearfully. What was it? She did not know; it was too subtle and elusive to name. But she felt it, creeping out of the sky, reaching toward her through the sounds, the scents, the color that filled the air.

Now her bosom rose and fell tumultuously. She was beginning to recognize this thing that was
approaching to possess her, and she was striving to beat it back with her will – as powerless as her
two white slender hands would have been.

When she abandoned herself a little whispered word escaped her slightly parted lips. She said it
over and over under her breath: "Free, free, free!" The vacant stare and the look of terror that had
followed it went from her eyes. They stayed keen and bright. Her pulses beat fast, and the coursing
blood warmed and relaxed every inch of her body.

She did not stop to ask if it were or were not a monstrous joy that held her. A clear and exalted
perception enabled her to dismiss the suggestion as trivial.

She knew that she would weep again when she saw the kind, tender hands folded in death; the
face that had never looked save with love upon her, fixed and gray and dead. But she saw beyond
that bitter moment a long procession of years to come that would belong to her absolutely. And she
opened and spread her arms out to them in welcome.

There would be no one to live for during those coming years; she would live for herself. There
would be no powerful will bending hers in that blind persistence with which men and women believe
they have a right to impose a private will upon a fellow-creature. A kind intention or a cruel intention
made the act seem no less a crime as she looked upon it in that brief moment of illumination.

And yet she had loved him – sometimes. Often she had not. What did it matter! What could love,
the unsolved mystery, count for in the face of this possession of self-assertion which she suddenly
recognized as the strongest impulse of her being!

"Free! Body and soul free!" she kept whispering.

Josephine was kneeling before the closed door with her lips to the keyhole, imploring for admission.

"Louise, open the door! I beg; open the door – you will make yourself ill. What are you doing,
Louise? For heaven's sake open the door."

"Go away. I am not making myself ill." No; she was drinking in a very elixir of life through that
open window.

Her fancy was running riot along those days ahead of her. Spring days, and summer days, and all
sorts of days that would be her own. She breathed a quick prayer that life might be long. It was only
yesterday she had thought with a shudder that life might be long.

She arose at length and opened the door to her sister's importunities. There was a feverish
triumph in her eyes, and she carried herself unwittingly like a goddess of Victory. She clasped her
sister's waist, and together they descended the stairs. Richards stood waiting for them at the bottom.

Someone was opening the front door with a latchkey. It was Brently Mallard who entered, a
little travel-stained, composedly carrying his grip-sack and umbrella. He had been far from the scene
of the accident, and did not even know there had been one. He stood amazed at Josephine's piercing
cry; at Richards' quick motion to screen him from the view of his wife.

But Richards was too late.

When the doctors came they said she had died of heart disease – of joy that kills.

1. List four things that Louise Mallard can see or hear through the window.

....

....

....

.... **[4 marks]**

2. Look in detail at lines 22 to 31 (*from* 'She was young…' *to* '…would have been'.)

How does the writer use language here to describe Louise Mallard's state of mind at this point in the story?

You could include the writer's choice of:
- words and phrases
- language features and techniques
- sentence forms. **[8 marks]**

3. Now think about the whole text.

This text is a complete short story.

How has the writer structured the story to interest and surprise you as a reader?

You could write about:
- what the writer focuses on at the beginning
- how and why she changes this focus
- the impact of the ending
- any other structural features that interest you. **[8 marks]**

4. Think about the whole text.

How does the writer present Louise Mallard and use her to express ideas about marriage and relationships?
- Write about your impressions of Louise Mallard and her reaction to the news of her husband's death.
- Evaluate how the writer has created these impressions.
- Support your opinions with quotations from the text. **[20 marks]**

Section B: Writing

You are advised to spend 45 minutes on this section: about 10 minutes planning, about 35 minutes writing.

5. **EITHER**

Choose one of the following titles for your writing:

a) Bad News

OR

b) Free, free, free!

OR

c) Write the opening of a story about a rail or car crash.

OR

d) Write about the world outside your window.

[24 marks for content and organisation and 16 marks for technical accuracy; total 40 marks]

END OF QUESTIONS

English Language Paper 2: Reading
Non-fiction and Non-fiction/Transactional Writing

Section A: Reading

Answer all questions in this section.

You are advised to spend 45 minutes on this section.

Source A is an extract from *Domestic Manners of the Americans* by Frances Trollope, published in 1832. In this chapter the writer, an Englishwoman living in the USA, gives her reaction to what she sees as the 'familiarity' of Americans.

The extraordinary familiarity of our poor neighbours startled us at first, and we hardly knew how to receive their uncouth advances, or what was expected of us in return; however, it sometimes produced very laughable scenes. Upon one occasion two of my children set off upon an exploring walk up the hills; they were absent rather longer than we expected, and the rest of our party

5   determined upon going out to meet them; we knew the direction they had taken, but thought it would be as well to enquire at a little public-house at the bottom of the hill, if such a pair had been seen to pass. A woman, whose appearance more resembled a Covent Garden market-woman than any thing else I can remember, came out and answered my question with the most jovial good humour in the affirmative, and prepared to join us in our search. Her look, her voice, her

10 manner, were so exceedingly coarse and vehement, that she almost frightened me; she passed her arm within mine, and to the inexpressible amusement of my young people, she dragged me on, talking and questioning me without ceasing. She lived but a short distance from us, and I am sure intended to be a very good neighbour; but her violent intimacy made me dread to pass her door; my children, including my sons, she always addressed by their Christian names, excepting when

15 she substituted the word "honey;" this familiarity of address, however, I afterwards found was universal throughout all ranks in the United States.

My general appellation amongst my neighbours was "the English old woman," but in mentioning each other they constantly employed the term "lady;" and they evidently had a pleasure in using it, for I repeatedly observed, that in speaking of a neighbour, instead of saying Mrs. Such-a-one,

20 they described her as "the lady over the way what takes in washing," or as "that there lady, out by the Gulley, what is making dip-candles." Mr. Trollope was as constantly called "the old man," while draymen, butchers' boys, and the labourers on the canal were invariably denominated "them gentlemen;" nay, we once saw one of the most gentlemanlike men in Cincinnati introduce a fellow in dirty shirt sleeves, and all sorts of detestable et cetera, to one of his friends, with this formula,

25 "D – let me introduce this gentleman to you." Our respective titles certainly were not very important; but the eternal shaking hands with these ladies and gentlemen was really an annoyance, and the more so, as the near approach of the gentlemen was always redolent of whiskey and tobacco.

Source B is an article in which the writer expresses his opinion about customer service in restaurants.

CALL ME (SIR OR) MADAM

Sean Boyle wants to be served by a waiter, not a new best friend.

'Hey, guys! How are you doing?'
The first time I was greeted like this by a waiter in a (fairly upmarket)
5 restaurant, I was outraged. Obviously not a very classy joint, I thought, and
not one I would care to set foot in again. But it's got to the point now that if
I stuck to my guns and boycotted every establishment where I was spoken to
like a New York delinquent rather than a middle-aged British gentleman, I
would never leave the house.
10   And what is it about the word 'guys'? Suddenly, it's everywhere, applied to people of both genders and
all ages. It started with children's T.V. presenters, ever notorious for using Americanisms to 'get down with
the kids', and now it's everywhere. On television it's used to address not just hip young men from the streets
but elderly ladies buying antiques, minor celebrities learning to dance and even elected politicians. Go into
any school nowadays and you're likely to hear the appalling Americanism 'Listen up, guys' rather than, 'Pay
15 attention, children' or 'Be quiet, Class Four'. Whenever more than one person is addressed they are called
'you guys'. It's as if nobody is aware that the plural form of the pronoun 'you' is 'you'.
    This kind of over-familiarity seems to have been imported from America – or copied from American
films and television. Yet – to bring us back to restaurants – friends who have lived in the USA tell me that
Americans are often more polite and formal than we are: being addressed as 'Sir' or 'Madam' is the norm.
20 Of course, you can get the forced friendliness of 'Hi, my name's Heidi. I'll be your server tonight.' That's
another irritating trend that's gaining a foothold over here – we don't need to know her name and we already
know what her job is. We're not here to get chummy with the staff; we just want them to bring us our food.
And when it happens in a British restaurant it just seems false. What we've imported is a stereotypical idea of
Stateside friendliness rather than genuine warmth and good manners.
25   I wonder if this need to embrace informality has something to do with a British dislike of servility. I used
to work in the service industry in London and – like most of my colleagues – was quite happy to address
customers as 'Sir' or 'Madam'. Yet I knew people who said they found this demeaning, as if by addressing
people in this way we were accepting that they were somehow superior to us.
    It has been said this discomfort with the idea of serving others is a reaction to the time when huge numbers
30 of working class Britons spent their lives 'in service', often in 'Downton Abbey' style big houses, where
they were never allowed to forget their lowly status. Twenty-first century Britons bow to no-one. In contrast,
in countries like France and Italy, serving people is not considered demeaning. To serve is not to be servile.
Walk into almost any restaurant in these countries and you will greeted by 'Bonjour' or 'Buona Sera' and
addressed as 'Monsieur/Madame' or 'Signore/Signora'. In return you are expected to greet not only the staff
35 but the people sitting near you. When you've done that, you can get on with eating your meal, efficiently
served by a professional waiter – not by your new best friend, Luigi.
    I don't want waiting staff and bar staff to touch their forelocks and grovel to me. But nor do I want my evening
out to turn into some kind of pseudo-American sitcom. There's a happy medium here, 'guys'. By all means be
friendly – there's nothing wrong with a cheerful smile as you say 'good evening' or even a brief chat about the
40 weather – but treat your customers with respect, starting with the use of 'Sir' and 'Madam'. And for the sake of
good customer relations, the English language and my blood pressure, please never, ever call us 'you guys'.

1. Read again the first paragraph of Source A (lines 1 to 16).

Choose four statements below which are TRUE.
- Shade the boxes of the ones that you think are true.
- Choose a maximum of four statements.

A. The neighbours are very unfriendly. ☐

B. Frances Trollope has more than two children. ☐

C. She knows which way the children went. ☐

D. The woman says she has not seen the children. ☐

E. The woman is quiet and gentle. ☐

F. Trollope's children find the incident funny. ☐

G. The neighbour calls Trollope's children by their first names. ☐

H. The woman's familiarity is unusual in America. ☐

[4 marks]

2. You need to refer to Source A and Source B for this question.

Use details from both sources. Write a summary of the differences and similarities between the behaviour described by Trollope and by Boyle. **[8 marks]**

3. You now need to refer only to Source A, the extract from *Domestic Manners of the Americans*.

How does the writer use language to inform and entertain the reader? **[12 marks]**

4. For this question you need to refer to both Source A and Source B.

Compare how the writers convey their attitudes to good manners and over-friendliness.

In your answer you should:
- Compare their attitudes.
- Compare the methods they use to convey these attitudes.
- Support your ideas with quotations from both texts. **[16 marks]**

Section B: Writing

You are advised to spend 45 minutes on this section.

You are reminded of the need to plan your answer.

You should write in full sentences.

You should leave enough time to check your work at the end.

5. 'People claim now that they have hundreds or even thousands of friends – but they've never met most of them. In real life nobody has more than two or three true friends.'

Write an article for a magazine in which you explain your point of view on this statement.

[24 marks for content and organisation and 16 marks for technical accuracy; total 40 marks]

END OF QUESTIONS

English Literature

There are four parts to the English Literature exam: Shakespeare; The Nineteenth Century Novel; Modern Texts; Poetry. The texts that each exam board offers for study are shown in the table below.

Exam Board	Exam		
	Shakespeare	**The Nineteenth Century Novel**	**Modern Texts**
AQA	• Macbeth • Romeo and Juliet • The Tempest • Much Ado About Nothing • The Merchant of Venice • Julius Caesar	• The Strange Case of Dr Jekyll and Mr Hyde • A Christmas Carol • Great Expectations • Jane Eyre • Frankenstein • Pride and Prejudice • The Sign of Four	• An Inspector Calls • Blood Brothers • The History Boys • DNA • The Curious Incident of the Dog in the Night-Time • A Taste of Honey • Lord of the Flies • Telling Tales • Animal Farm • Never Let Me Go • Anita and Me • Pigeon English
Edexcel	• Macbeth • Romeo and Juliet • The Tempest • Much Ado About Nothing • The Merchant of Venice • Twelfth Night	• The Strange Case of Dr Jekyll and Mr Hyde • A Christmas Carol • Great Expectations • Jane Eyre • Frankenstein • Pride and Prejudice • Silas Marner	• An Inspector Calls • Blood Brothers • Lord of the Flies • Animal Farm • Anita and Me • The Woman in Black • Hobson's Choice • Journey's End
OCR	• Macbeth • Romeo and Juliet • Much Ado About Nothing • The Merchant of Venice	• The Strange Case of Dr Jekyll and Mr Hyde • Great Expectations • Jane Eyre • Pride and Prejudice • The War of the Worlds	• An Inspector Calls • DNA • Animal Farm • Never Let Me Go • Anita and Me • My Mother Said I Never Should
WJEC Eduqas	• Macbeth • Romeo and Juliet • Much Ado About Nothing • The Merchant of Venice • Henry V • Othello	• The Strange Case of Dr Jekyll and Mr Hyde • A Christmas Carol • Jane Eyre • Pride and Prejudice • Silas Marner • The War of the Worlds	• An Inspector Calls • Blood Brothers • The History Boys • The Curious Incident of the Dog in the Night-Time • A Taste of Honey • Lord of the Flies • Never Let Me Go • Anita and Me • The Woman in Black • Oranges Are Not the Only Fruit

Please note that line numbers given in the questions in the following pages may vary, according to which edition of the text you are using.

English Literature Practice Papers Set A

Pages 24–27: English Literature: Shakespeare

The questions on pages 24–27 will help you to revise for:

- AQA Paper 1
- Edexcel Paper 1
- OCR Paper 2
- WJEC Eduqas Component 1

Answer one question from this section on the play you have studied.

The marks for the questions are shown in brackets.

Pages 28–32: English Literature: The Nineteenth Century Novel

The questions on pages 28–32 will help you to revise for:

- AQA Paper 1
- Edexcel Paper 2
- OCR Paper 1
- WJEC Eduqas Component 2

Answer one question from this section on the novel you have studied.

The marks for the questions are shown in brackets.

Pages 33–36: English Literature: Modern Texts

The questions on pages 33–36 will help you to revise for:

- AQA Paper 2
- Edexcel Paper 1
- OCR Paper 1
- WJEC Eduqas Component 2

Answer one question from this section on the text you have studied.

The marks for the questions are shown in brackets.

Pages 37–40: English Literature: Poetry and Unseen Poetry

The poetry questions on pages 37–38 will help you to revise for:

- AQA Paper 2
- Edexcel Paper 2
- OCR Paper 2
- WJEC Eduqas Component 1

The unseen poetry questions on pages 39–40 will help you to revise for:

- AQA Paper 2
- Edexcel Paper 2
- WJEC Eduqas Component 2

The marks for the questions are shown in brackets.

Name: ....

English Literature: Shakespeare

Answer the question on the play you have studied.

You should spend between 40 and 55 minutes answering the question.

1. *Macbeth*

   Read the extract and then answer the question that follows:

Act 4 Scene 3, lines 214–236: Here, Malcolm has just told Macduff that his family has been killed on Macbeth's orders.

   Read from

   MALCOLM   Be comforted

   to

   MACDUFF   Within my sword's length set him. If he 'scape,
                      Heaven forgive him too.

   Starting with this extract, explore how Shakespeare presents Macduff's character.

   Write about:
   - how Shakespeare presents Macduff in this extract
   - how Shakespeare presents Macduff in the play as a whole. **[40 marks]**

2. *Romeo and Juliet*

   Read the extract and then answer the question that follows:

Act 2 Scene 3, lines 65–93: Here, Friar Laurence reacts to the news that Romeo has fallen in love with Juliet.

   Read from

   FRIAR LAURENCE   Holy Saint Francis, what a change is here!

   to

   FRIAR LAURENCE   Wisely and slow. They stumble that run fast.
                                    Exeunt

   Starting with this extract, explore how Shakespeare presents attitudes to love in *Romeo and Juliet*.

   Write about:
   - how Shakespeare presents attitudes to love in this extract
   - how Shakespeare presents attitudes to love in the whole play. **[40 marks]**

3. *The Tempest*

Read the extract and then answer the question that follows:

> **Act 2 Scene 2, lines 166–186: In this scene Stefano and Trinculo have made Caliban drunk and he has sworn to serve Stefano instead of Prospero.**
>
> **Read from**
> CALIBAN   I prithee, let me bring thee where crabs grow…
>
> **to**
>
> CALIBAN   Freedom, high-day! High-day, freedom! Freedom, high-day, freedom!

Starting with this speech, explain how Shakespeare writes about slavery and freedom in *The Tempest*.

Write about:
- how Shakespeare presents ideas about slavery and freedom in this extract
- how Shakespeare presents ideas about slavery and freedom in the play as a whole.   **[40 marks]**

4. *Much Ado about Nothing*

Read the extract and then answer the question that follows:

> **Act 1 Scene 3, lines 12–35: Here, Don John discusses his sad mood and discontent with Conrad.**
>
> **Read from**
> DON JOHN   I cannot hide what I am.
>
> **to**
>
> CONRAD   Can you make no use of your discontent?

Starting with this extract, explore how Shakespeare presents the character of Don John in *Much Ado about Nothing*.

Write about:
- how Shakespeare presents Don John in this extract
- how Shakespeare presents Don John in the play as a whole.   **[40 marks]**

5. *The Merchant of Venice*

Read the extract and then answer the question that follows:

> **Act 3 Scene 2, lines 1–24: Here, Portia explains her feelings to Bassanio before he chooses a casket.**
>
> **Read from**
> PORTIA   I pray you tarry. Pause a day or two
>
> **to**
>
> PORTIA   I speak too long, but 'tis to pieze the time,
>   To eke it, and to draw it out in length
>   To stay you from election.

Starting with this speech, explore how Shakespeare presents the role of women in *The Merchant of Venice*.

Write about:
- how Shakespeare writes about the role of women in this speech
- how Shakespeare writes about the role of women in the play as a whole.   **[40 marks]**

6. **Julius Caesar**

   Read the extract and then answer the question that follows:

Act 5 Scene 5, lines 63–80: After losing the final battle, Brutus has killed himself.
Read from
MESSALA How died my master, Strato?
to
OCTAVIUS So call the field to rest, and let's away
To part the glories of this happy day.

   Starting with this speech, explore how Shakespeare presents Brutus as 'the noblest Roman of them all' in *Julius Caesar*.

   Write about:
   - how Shakespeare presents Brutus in this speech
   - how Shakespeare presents Brutus in the play as a whole. **[40 marks]**

7. **Henry V**

   Read the extract and then answer both parts of the question that follows:

Act 1 Prologue, lines 1–34: At the start of the play the Chorus addresses the audience.
Read from
CHORUS O for a Muse of fire, that would ascend
The brightest heaven of invention:
to
CHORUS Who, prologue-like your humble patience pray
Gently to hear, kindly to judge, our play.
Exit

   a) Look at how the Chorus speaks and acts here.

      How would an audience respond to this part of the play? Refer closely to the extract to support your answer.

   b) Write about how Shakespeare presents Henry V as an important figure in the history of England at different points in the play. **[40 marks]**

8. *Othello*

Read the extract and then answer both parts of the question that follows:

> **Act 2 Scene 1, lines 285–311: In this speech Iago tells the audience of his plans to make Othello jealous.**
>
> **Read from**
>
> IAGO   That Cassio loves her, I do well believe it.
>
> **to**
>
> IAGO   Knavery's plain face is never seen till used.

a) Look at how Iago speaks and acts here.

   How would an audience respond to this part of the play? Refer closely to the extract to support your answer.

b) Write about how Shakespeare presents the theme of jealousy at different points in the play.

   [40 marks]

9. *Twelfth Night*

Read the extract and then answer both parts of the question that follows:

> **Act 2 Scene 4, lines 92–122: Here, Orsino tells Viola that women cannot love as strongly as men do.**
>
> **Read from**
>
> ORSINO   There is no woman's sides
>
>   Can bide the beating of so strong a passion
>
>   As love doth give my heart;
>
> **to**
>
> VIOLA   I am all the daughters of my father's house,
>
>   And all the brothers too; and yet I know not.
>
>   Sir, Shall I to this lady?

a) Explore how Shakespeare writes about unrequited love in this extract.

b) Explain how Shakespeare writes about unrequited love elsewhere in the play.

   You should refer to the context of the play in your answer.

   [40 marks]

English Literature: The Nineteenth Century Novel

Answer the question on the novel you have studied.

You should spend between 45 and 55 minutes on the question.

1. **Robert Louis Stevenson:** *The Strange Case of Dr Jekyll and Mr Hyde*

   Answer both parts of the question.

   > **Read Chapter 10 ('Henry Jekyll's Full Statement of the Case') from**
   > I hesitated long before I put this theory to the test of practice.
   > **to**
   > I stole through the corridors, a stranger in my own house; and coming into my room, I saw for the first time the appearance of Edward Hyde.

   In this extract, Jekyll describes how he first experimented on himself and turned into Mr Hyde.

   Starting with this extract, write about how Stevenson explores ideas about scientific discovery and experimentation in *The Strange Case of Dr Jekyll and Mr Hyde*.

   Write about:
   - how Stevenson writes about Jekyll's actions as seen in this extract
   - how he uses the 'strange case' to explore ideas about the possibilities and dangers of science in the novel as a whole. **[40 marks]**

2. **Charles Dickens:** *A Christmas Carol*

   Answer both parts of the question.

   > **Read Stave (Chapter) 2 ('The First of the Three Spirits') from**
   > 'Are you the Spirit, sir, whose coming was foretold to me?' asked Scrooge.
   > **to**
   > He was conscious of a thousand odours floating in the air, each one connected with a thousand thoughts, and hopes, and joys, and cares long, long, forgotten.

   In this extract, the Ghost of Christmas Past appears to Scrooge and takes him on a journey into the past.

   Starting with this extract, explain how Dickens writes about how Scrooge has been shaped by his experiences.

   Write about:
   - how Dickens writes about Scrooge and the Ghost of Christmas Past in this extract
   - how he explores how his experiences have shaped Scrooge's character elsewhere in the novel. **[40 marks]**

3. **Charles Dickens: _Great Expectations_**

    Answer both parts of the question.

    > **Read Chapter 18 from**
    >
    > At those times I would get up and look out at the door; for, our kitchen door opened at once upon the night, and stood open on summer evenings to air the room.
    >
    > **to**
    >
    > It was furnished with fresh young remembrances too, and even at the same moment I fell into much the same confused division of mind between it and the better rooms to which I was going, as I had been so often between the forge and Miss Havisham's, and Biddy and Estella.

    In this extract, Pip, Joe and Biddy discuss Pip's plans for buying new clothes before he leaves for London.

    Starting with this extract, write about how Dickens uses Pip to explore ideas about social class.

    Write about:
    *   how differences in social class and Pip's attitude to them are shown in this extract
    *   how Dickens uses Pip to explore social class and attitudes to it elsewhere in the novel.

    [40 marks]

4. **Charlotte Brontë: _Jane Eyre_**

    Answer both parts of the question.

    > **Read Chapter 26 from**
    >
    > And now I can recall the picture of the gray old house of God rising calm before me, of a rook wheeling round the steeple, of a ruddy morning sky beyond.
    >
    > **to**
    >
    > 'the marriage cannot go on: I declare the existence of an impediment.'

    In this extract, Jane and Rochester are about to be married when the ceremony is interrupted.

    Starting with this extract, write about how Brontë presents faith and religion, and their importance to Jane Eyre.

    Write about:
    *   how Brontë writes about the church and the wedding ceremony in this extract
    *   how Brontë writes about faith and religion in the novel as a whole.

    [40 marks]

5. **Mary Shelley: *Frankenstein***

Answer both parts of the question.

> **Read Chapter 10 from**
> The ascent is precipitous, but the path is cut into continual and short windings, which enable you to surmount the perpendicularity of the mountain.
> **to**
> ...but now we are moved by every wind that blows and a chance word or scene that that word may convey to us.

In this extract Victor Frankenstein seeks comfort in nature as he climbs mount Montanvert.

Starting with this extract, write about how Shelley writes about nature.

Write about:
*   how Shelley writes about nature in this extract
*   how Shelley writes about nature and attitudes to nature in the novel as a whole.   **[40 marks]**

6. **Jane Austen: *Pride and Prejudice***

Answer both parts of the question.

> **Read Chapter 23 from**
> Mrs Bennet was in fact too much overpowered to say a great deal while Sir William remained; but no sooner had he left them than her feelings found a rapid vent.
> **to**
> ...it gratified him, he said, to discover that Charlotte Lucas, whom he had been used to think tolerably sensible, was as foolish as his wife, and more foolish than his daughter!

In this extract, Mr and Mrs Bennet react to the news that Charlotte Lucas is to be married to Mr Collins.

Starting with this extract, explore how Austen writes about the Bennets as parents in *Pride and Prejudice*.

Write about:
*   how Austen writes about Mr and Mrs Bennet as parents in this extract
*   how Austen writes about Mr and Mrs Bennet as parents in the novel as a whole.   **[40 marks]**

7. **Sir Arthur Conan Doyle: *The Sign of Four***

Answer both parts of the question.

> **Read Chapter 1 from**
>
> 'The only unofficial consulting detective,' he answered. 'I am the last and highest court of appeal in detection.'
>
> **to**
>
> I had a Jezail bullet through it some time before, and, though it did not prevent me from walking, it ached wearily at every change in the weather.

In this extract, Holmes and Watson discuss Holmes's career and Watson's account of one of his cases.

Starting with this extract, explore how Conan Doyle uses Watson as a narrator in *The Sign of Four.*

Write about:
- how Conan Doyle uses Watson as a narrator in this extract
- how Conan Doyle uses Watson as a narrator in the novel as a whole.   **[40 marks]**

8. **H. G. Wells: *The War of the Worlds***

> **Read Book 1 Chapter 16 from**
>
> So you understand the roaring wave of fear that swept through the greatest city in the world just as Monday was dawning - the stream of flight rising swiftly to a torrent, lashing in a foaming tumult round the railway stations, banked up into a horrible struggle about the shipping in the Thames, and hurrying by every available channel northwards and eastward.
>
> **to**
>
> Another bank drove over Ealing, and surrounded a little island of survivors on Castle Hill, alive, but unable to escape.

Use this extract and your knowledge of the whole novel to answer this question.

Write about how Wells presents the experience of people fleeing from the Martians.

In your response you should:
- refer to the extract and the novel as a whole
- show your understanding of characters and events in the novel
- refer to the context of the novel.   **[40 marks]**

9. **George Eliot:** *Silas Marner*

> **Read Chapter 19 from**
>
> 'I can never be sorry, father,' said Eppie. 'I shouldn't know what to think or to wish for with fine things about me, as I haven't been used to.'
>
> **to**
>
> In this way she covered her husband's abrupt departure, for Godfrey had gone straight to the door, unable to say more.

Use this extract and your knowledge of the whole novel to answer this question.

Write about how Eliot presents Godfrey Cass as a father and a husband.

In your response you should:
* refer to the extract and the novel as a whole
* show your understanding of characters and events in the novel
* refer to the context of the novel.

[40 marks]

English Literature: Modern Texts

Answer one question on the text you have studied.

You should spend between 45 and 55 minutes on the question.

1. **J. B. Priestley: *An Inspector Calls***

   How does Priestley write about social problems in *An Inspector Calls*?

   Write about:
   - the social problems that Priestley writes about in *An Inspector Calls*
   - how Priestley presents these problems by the way he writes.   **[40 marks]**

2. **Willy Russell: *Blood Brothers***

   Do Mickey and his mother create their own tragedy in *Blood Brothers* or are they just victims?

   Write about:
   - what Mickey and Mrs Johnstone do and what happens to them
   - how Russell writes about what they do and what happens to them.   **[40 marks]**

3. **Alan Bennett: *The History Boys***

   How does Bennett use the Headmaster to present ideas about education and authority in *The History Boys*?

   Write about:
   - what the Headmaster does and says
   - how Bennett presents the Headmaster in the play.   **[40 marks]**

4. **Dennis Kelly: *DNA***

   How does Kelly write about the way teenagers can behave in *DNA*?

   Write about:
   - the actions taken by the teenage characters in *DNA*
   - how Kelly presents their actions in the play.   **[40 marks]**

5. **Simon Stephens: *The Curious Incident of the Dog in the Night-Time***

   How does Stephens present the character Christopher as being different from other people in *The Curious Incident of the Dog in the Night-Time*?

   Write about:
   - things Christopher does and says that indicate his 'difference'
   - how Stephens presents Christopher as being different from other characters.   **[40 marks]**

6. **Shelagh Delaney: *A Taste of Honey***

How does Delaney write about women's attitudes towards men in *A Taste of Honey*?

Write about:
- how Delaney presents male characters and what they say and do
- how Helen and Jo react to and talk about men. **[40 marks]**

7. **William Golding: *Lord of the Flies***

Is Simon an important character in *Lord of the Flies*?

Write about:
- how Golding presents the character of Simon
- the significance of Simon in *Lord of the Flies*. **[40 marks]**

8. **AQA Anthology: *Telling Tales***

How do writers explore relationships between people of different generations in 'Korea' and one other story from *Telling Tales*?

Write about:
- the relationships described in the two stories
- how the writers present these relationships. **[40 marks]**

9. **George Orwell: *Animal Farm***

How does Orwell use old Major and his dream to write about idealism?

Write about:
- how Orwell presents old Major's ideals
- how Orwell uses old Major's ideals to explore the results and limits of idealism. **[40 marks]**

10. **Kazuo Ishiguro: *Never Let Me Go***

How does Ishiguro present Kathy and what difference does her role as narrator make to our reading of *Never Let Me Go*?

Write about:
- how Ishiguro presents Kathy's character in *Never Let Me Go*
- how he uses language as the narrator of *Never Let Me Go*. **[40 marks]**

11. **Meera Syal: *Anita and Me***

How does Syal present Indian culture and tradition in *Anita and Me*?

Write about:
- examples of Indian culture and traditions in *Anita and Me*
- how Syal writes about Indian culture and traditions. **[40 marks]**

12. **Stephen Kelman: *Pigeon English***

How does Kelman present violence and danger in *Pigeon English*?

Write about:
- examples of violent and dangerous behaviour in *Pigeon English*
- how Kelman presents violent and dangerous behaviour.

[40 marks]

13. **Harold Brighouse: *Hobson's Choice***

I'm value to you, so's my man; and you can boast it at the 'Moonraker's' that your daughter Maggie's made the strangest, finest match a woman's made this fifty year.

Explore the relationship between Maggie and Willie and how it changes during the course of the play.

You must refer to the context of the play in your answer.

[40 marks]

14. **R. C. Sherriff: *Journey's End***

Supposing the worst happened - supposing we were knocked right out. Think of all the chaps who've gone already. It can't be very lonely there - with all those fellows. Sometimes I think it's lonelier here.

Journey's End has been described as an 'anti-war' play. To what extent and in what ways do you agree with this description of the play?

You must refer to the context of the play in your answer.

[40 marks]

15. **Charlotte Keatley: *My Mother Said I Never Should***

Re-read Act Three Scene Eight and answer both parts of the question.

a) How does Keatley explore Doris's feelings about marriage and work in this extract?

b) Write about how she explores changing attitudes to marriage and work in another part of the play.

[40 marks]

16. **Susan Hill: *The Woman in Black***

Read 'Whistle and I'll Come to You' from the start of the chapter to

Then yes, again, a cry, that familiar cry of desperation and anguish, a cry for help from a child somewhere out on the marsh.

Use this extract and your knowledge of the whole novel to answer this question.

How does Hill use places to create atmosphere in *The Woman in Black*?

In your response you should:
- refer to the extract and the novel as a whole
- show your understanding of characters and events in the novel.

[40 marks]

17. **Jeanette Winterson: *Oranges Are Not the Only Fruit***

Read 'Genesis' from

Sunday was the Lord's day, the most vigorous day of the whole week; we had a radiogram at home with an imposing mahogany front and a fat Bakelite knob to twiddle for the stations.

to

'Who was the oldest man in the Bible?'

Use this extract and your knowledge of the whole novel to answer the question.

How does Winterson write about the part played by religion in Jeanette's life in *Oranges Are Not the Only Fruit*?

In your response you should:
- refer to the extract and the novel as a whole
- show your understanding of characters and events in the novel.

[40 marks]

English Literature: Poetry and Unseen Poetry

Answer the question(s) for the exam board you are studying.

AQA Anthology

You should spend between 35 and 45 minutes on this question.

EITHER

1. Compare the way poets present ideas about memories in 'Eden Rock' and one other poem from 'Love and Relationships'.   **[20 marks]**

OR

2. Compare the way poets write about war in 'Bayonet Charge' and one other poem from 'Power and Conflict'.   **[20 marks]**

Edexcel Anthology

You are advised to spend about 35 minutes on this question.

EITHER

3. Read 'A Complaint'. Choose one other poem from 'Relationships'. Compare how the poets use imagery to express their feelings in the two poems.

   In your answer you should consider:
   - the poets' use of language, form and structure
   - the influence of the contexts in which the poems were written.   **[20 marks]**

OR

4. Read 'Belfast Confetti'. Choose one other poem from 'Conflict'. Compare how the poets present violent events in both poems.

   In your answer you should consider:
   - the poets' use of language, form and structure
   - the influence of the contexts in which the poems were written.   **[20 marks]**

OR

5. Read 'Absence'. Choose one other poem from 'Time and Place'. Compare how the poets use descriptions of places to express their moods and feelings in both poems.

   In your answer you should consider:
   - the poets' use of language, form and structure
   - the influence of the contexts in which the poems were written.   **[20 marks]**

WJEC Eduqas Anthology

6. Answer both part (a) and part (b).

You are advised to spend about 20 minutes on part (a) and about 40 minutes on part (b).

   a) Read 'Afternoons' by Philip Larkin.
     In this poem Larkin writes about the effects of passing time on people's lives. Write about the way Larkin presents the passing time in this poem.
   b) Choose another poem from the anthology in which the poet also writes about time. Compare the presentation of passing time in your chosen poem to the presentation of passing time in 'Afternoons'.

In your answer to part (b) you should compare:
- the content and structure of the poems - what they are about and how they are organised
- how the writers create effects, using appropriate terminology where relevant
- the contexts of the poems, and how these may have influenced the ideas in them.   **[20 marks]**

OCR Anthology

EITHER

7. Love and Relationships

Read 'Love After Love' and 'Past and Present' (on page 39) and then answer both parts of the question.
   a) Compare how the poets express feelings about the past.   **[20 marks]**
   b) Explore in detail how one other poem from the anthology presents feelings about the past.   **[20 marks]**

OR

8. Conflict

Read 'There's a certain slant of light' and 'Past and Present' (on page 39) and then answer both parts of the question.
   a) Compare how the poems present feelings about death and mortality.   **[20 marks]**
   b) Explore in detail one other poem from the anthology which presents feelings about death and mortality.   **[20 marks]**

OR

9. Youth and Age

Read 'Cold Knap Lake' and 'Past and Present' (on page 39) and then answer both parts of the question.
   a) Compare how the poets write about childhood.   **[20 marks]**
   b) Explore in detail one other poem from the anthology that presents ideas and feelings about childhood.   **[20 marks]**

Unseen Poetry

Answer both questions.

You should spend a total of between 40 and 50 minutes on both questions.

1. Read 'Past and Present' by Thomas Hood.

Past and Present

I remember, I remember
The house where I was born,
The little window where the sun
Came peeping in at morn;
He never came a wink too soon
Nor brought too long a day;
But now, I often wish the night
Had borne my breath away.

I remember, I remember
The roses, red and white,
The violets and the lily-cups-
Those flowers made of light!
The lilacs where the robin built,
And where my brother set
The laburnum on his birthday,-
The tree is living yet!

I remember, I remember
Where I was used to swing,
And thought the air must rush as fresh
To swallows on the wing;
My spirit flew in feathers then
That is so heavy now,
And summer pools could hardly cool
The fever on my brow.

I remember, I remember
The fir trees dark and high;
I used to think their slender tops
Were close against the sky:
It was a childish ignorance,
But now 'tis little joy
To know I'm farther off from Heaven
Than when I was a boy.

                    Thomas Hood

a) In 'Past and Present' how does the poet present his feelings about his childhood?

b) Now read 'The Swing' by Robert Louis Stevenson.

The Swing

How do you like to go up in a swing,
Up in the air so blue?
Oh, I do think it the pleasantest thing
Ever a child can do!

Up in the air and over the wall,
Till I can see so wide,
River and trees and cattle and all
Over the countryside--

Till I look down on the garden green,
Down on the roof so brown--
Up in the air I go flying again,
Up in the air and down!
     Robert Louis Stevenson

In both 'Past and Present' and 'The Swing' the poets write about children. What are the similarities and or/ differences between the ways the poets present their feelings? **[20 marks]**

END OF QUESTIONS

English Literature Practice Papers Set B

Pages 42–46: English Literature: Shakespeare

The questions on pages 42–46 will help you to revise for:

- AQA Paper 1
- Edexcel Paper 1
- OCR Paper 2
- WJEC Eduqas Component 1

Answer one question from this section on the play you have studied.

The marks for the questions are shown in brackets.

Pages 47–50: English Literature: The Nineteenth Century Novel

The questions on pages 47–50 will help you to revise for:

- AQA Paper 1
- Edexcel Paper 2
- OCR Paper 1
- WJEC Eduqas Component 2

Answer one question from this section on the novel you have studied.

The marks for the questions are shown in brackets.

Pages 51–55: English Literature: Modern Texts

The questions on pages 51–55 will help you to revise for:

- AQA Paper 2
- Edexcel Paper 1
- OCR Paper 1
- WJEC Eduqas Component 2

Answer one question from this section on the text you have studied.

The marks for the questions are shown in brackets.

Pages 56–59: English Literature: Poetry and Unseen Poetry

The poetry questions on pages 56–57 will help you to revise for:

- AQA Paper 2
- Edexcel Paper 2
- OCR Paper 2
- WJEC Eduqas Component 1

The unseen poetry questions on pages 58–59 will help you to revise for:

- AQA Paper 2
- Edexcel Paper 2
- WJEC Eduqas Component 2

The marks for the questions are shown in brackets.

Name: _____

English Literature: Shakespeare

Answer the question on the play you have studied.

You should spend between 40 and 55 minutes answering the question.

1. *Macbeth*

   Read the extract and then answer both parts of the question that follows:

   > **Act 3 Scene 4, lines 121–143: In this extract, Macbeth talks to Lady Macbeth after seeing the ghost of Banquo.**
   >
   > **Read from**
   > MACBETH   It will have blood, they say. Blood will have blood.
   > **to**
   > MACBETH   We are yet but young in deed.
   >   *Exeunt*

   a) Explore how Shakespeare shows Macbeth becoming more ruthless and tyrannical in this extract. Refer closely to the extract in your answer.

   b) In this extract Macbeth shows that he has changed. Explain how Macbeth changes from loyal subject to ruthless tyrant during the course of the play.

      In your answer you must consider:
      • how he changes
      • why he changes.

      You should refer to the context of the play in your answer.   **[40 marks]**

2. **Romeo and Juliet**

Read the extract and then answer both parts of the question that follows:

Act 4 Scene 3, lines 29–57: In this extract Juliet takes the poison that she has been given by Friar Laurence.

Read from

JULIET	How if, when I am laid into the tomb,
	I wake before the time that Romeo
	Come to redeem me?
to	
JULIET	Romeo, Romeo, Romeo! Here's drink. I drink to thee.

*She drinks from the vial
and falls upon the bed.*

---

a) Explore how Shakespeare presents the character of Juliet in this extract. Refer closely to the extract in your answer.

b) In this extract Juliet imagines waking up among the dead in the family tomb. Explain how love and death are linked elsewhere in the play.

In your answer you must consider:
- how love and death are linked
- the effects of the link between love and death.

You should refer to the context of the play in your answer. **[40 marks]**

3. **The Tempest**

Read the extract and then answer both parts of the question that follows:

Act 3 Scene 1, lines 38–59: In this scene Ferdinand and Miranda speak about their feelings for each other.

Read from

FERDINAND	Admired Miranda!
to	
MIRANDA	But I prattle
	Something too wildly and my father's precepts
	I therein do forget.

---

a) Explore how Shakespeare presents the love between Ferdinand and Miranda in this extract. Refer closely to the extract in your answer.

b) In this extract Ferdinand and Miranda talk about love. Explain the importance of love elsewhere in the play.

In your answer you must consider:
- how love is presented
- how love affects the characters.

You should refer to the context of the play in your answer. **[40 marks]**

4. **Much Ado about Nothing**

Read the extract and then answer the question that follows:

Act 3 Scene 1, lines 81–116: Hero and Ursula are playing a trick on Beatrice, talking about Benedick's feelings when they know she is listening.

Read from

HERO   No. Rather will I go to Benedick

                And counsel him to fight against his passion.

to

BEATRICE   For others say thou dost deserve, and I

                Believe it better than reportingly.

                                Exit

Explore the use of trickery and deception in *Much Ado about Nothing*. Refer to this extract and elsewhere in the play.   **[40 marks]**

5. **The Merchant of Venice**

Read the extract and then answer the question that follows:

Act 2 Scene 5, lines 28–56: Here Shylock advises Jessica to lock herself in during the masque, not knowing that she has plans to elope with a Christian.

Read from

SHYLOCK   What, are there masques?

to

JESSICA   Farewell; and if my fortune be not crossed,

              I have a father, you a daughter lost.

                            Exit

Explore whether audiences would sympathise with Shylock and whether their attitudes might change during the play. Refer to this extract and elsewhere in the play.   **[40 marks]**

6. *Julius Caesar*

    Read the extract and then answer the question that follows:

Act 4 Scene 2, lines 53–79 (also referred to as Act 4, Scene 3, lines 1–28): In this scene Cassius and Brutus argue about Brutus's punishment of one of their followers for taking bribes.
Read from
CASSIUS   That you have wronged me doth appear in this:
to
BRUTUS   I had rather be a dog and bay the moon   Than such a Roman.

    Starting with this speech, explore how Shakespeare presents the relationship between Cassius and Brutus. Write about:
    *   how Shakespeare presents Cassius and Brutus in this extract
    *   how Shakespeare presents their relationship in the play as a whole. **[40 marks]**

7. *Henry V*

    Read the extract and then answer both parts of the question that follows:

Act 4 Scene 7, lines 64–87: Here, a French herald asks for permission to collect the dead from the battlefield and Henry realises he has won the battle.
Read from
EXETER   Here comes the herald of the French, my liege.
to
MONTJOY   They call it Agincourt.

    a) How does Shakespeare use this conversation to create a sense of the experience of war? Refer closely to the extract to support your answer.

    b) Write about how Shakespeare presents the effects of war at different points in the play. **[40 marks]**

8. *Othello*

Read the extract and then answer both parts of the question that follows:

> **Act 3 Scene 3, lines 76–93: In this speech Iago tells the audience of his plans to make Othello jealous.**
>
> **Read from**
>
> OTHELLO   Prithee, no more. Let him come when he will.
>
>   I will deny thee nothing.
>
> **to**
>
> OTHELLO   Excellent wretch! Perdition catch my soul
>
>   But I do love thee, and when I love thee not,
>
>   Chaos is come again.

a) Look at how Othello and Desdemona speak and act here. How would an audience respond to this part of the play? Refer closely to the extract to support your answer.

b) Write about how Shakespeare presents ideas about marriage at different points in the play.

[40 marks]

9. *Twelfth Night*

Read the extract and then answer both parts of the question that follows:

> **Act 1 Scene 1, lines 1–22: At the beginning of the play, Orsino speaks to Curio about his love for Olivia.**
>
> **Read from**
>
> ORSINO   If music be the food of love, play on.
>
>   Give me excess of it, that, surfeiting,
>
>   The appetite may sicken, and so die.
>
> **to**
>
>   *Enter Valentine*
>
> ORSINO   How now! What news from her?

a) Explore how Shakespeare writes about love in this extract. Refer closely to the extract in your answer.

b) Explain how Shakespeare writes about love elsewhere in the play.

In your answer you must consider:
* how love is shown
* the effect of love on the characters.

You should refer to the context of the play in your answer.

[40 marks]

English Literature: The Nineteenth Century Novel

Answer the question on the novel you have studied.

You should spend between 45 and 55 minutes on the question.

1. **Robert Louis Stevenson: *The Strange Case of Dr Jekyll and Mr Hyde***

> **Read Chapter 7 ('Incident at the Window') from**
>
> *The court was very cool and a little damp, and full of premature twilight, although the sky, high up overhead, was still bright with sunset.*
>
> **to**
>
> *But Mr Enfield only nodded his head very seriously, and walked on once more in silence.*

You should use this extract and your knowledge of the whole novel to answer this question.

Write about how sympathetically Jekyll is presented at different points in the novel.

In your response you should:
- refer to the extract and the novel as a whole
- show your understanding of the characters and events in the novel
- refer to the contexts of the novel. **[40 marks]**

2. **Charles Dickens: *A Christmas Carol***

> **Read Stave (Chapter) 4 ('The Last of the Spirits') from**
>
> *She hurried out to meet him; and Bob in his comforter – he had need of it, poor fellow – came in.*
>
> **to**
>
> *'I'm sure he's a good soul,' said Mrs Cratchit.*

You should use this extract and your knowledge of the whole novel to answer this question.

Write about the role and significance of the Cratchit family in *A Christmas Carol*.

In your response you should:
- refer to the extract and the novel as a whole
- show your understanding of the characters and events in the novel
- refer to the contexts of the novel. **[40 marks]**

3. **Charles Dickens: *Great Expectations***

Answer both parts of the question.

> **Read Chapter 1 from**
>
> *'Hold your noise!' cried a terrible voice, as a man started up from among the graves at the side of the church porch.*
>
> **to**
>
> *'Darn me if I couldn't eat em,' said the man, with a threatening shake of his head, 'and if I han't half a mind to't!'*

In this extract Pip meets Magwitch for the first time.

a) Explore how Dickens presents Magwitch and the impression he makes on Pip. Give examples from the extract to support your ideas.

b) In this extract Pip describes his first reaction to Magwitch. Explain the role played by Magwitch **elsewhere** in the novel.

In your answer you must consider:
  • how Magwitch acts
  • the effect of his actions on Pip.   **[40 marks]**

4. **Charlotte Brontë: *Jane Eyre***

> **Read Chapter 17 from**
>
> *'Now is my time to slip away,' thought I: but the tones that then severed the air arrested me.*
>
> **to**
>
> *He stopped, but his lip, and abruptly left me.*

You should use this extract and your knowledge of the whole novel to answer this question.

Write about how Jane's position as a governess and her awareness of social class are explored at different points in the novel.

In your response you should:
  • refer to the extract and the novel as a whole
  • show your understanding of the characters and events in the novel
  • refer to the contexts of the novel.   **[40 marks]**

5. **Mary Shelley: *Frankenstein***

Answer both parts of the question.

> **Read Chapter 4 from**
>
> *No-one can conceive the variety of feelings which bore me onwards, like a hurricane, in the first enthusiasm of success.*
>
> **to**
>
> *The dissecting room and the slaughter-house furnished many of my materials; and often did my human nature turn with loathing from my occupation, whilst, still urged on by an eagerness which perpetually increased, I brought my work near to a conclusion.*

In this extract Frankenstein describes his work as he begins to create the creature.

a) Explore how Shelley presents Frankenstein's feelings about his work.
Give examples from the extract to support your ideas.

b) In this extract Frankenstein thinks about the significance of his work. Explain how
Shelley writes about Frankenstein's feelings about his work **elsewhere** in the novel.

In your answer you must consider:
- what he says about the results of his work
- what this tells us about his character and how he changes. **[40 marks]**

6. **Jane Austen: *Pride and Prejudice***

> **Read Chapter 29 (Vol. 2 Chapter 6) from**
>
> *Mr Collins's triumph in consequence of this invitation was complete.*
>
> **to**
>
> *'Lady Catherine will not think the worse of you for being simply dressed. She likes to have the distinction of rank preserved.'*

In this extract, Mr Collins expresses his delight at receiving an invitation from
Lady Catherine de Burgh.

Explore how Austen writes about snobbery in *Pride and Prejudice*, in this extract
and elsewhere in the novel. **[40 marks]**

7. **Sir Arthur Conan Doyle: *The Sign of Four***

> **Read Chapter 11 from**
>
> *'That is all over,' I answered. 'It was nothing. I will tell you no more gloomy details.'*
>
> **to**
>
> *'Then I say, "Thank God" too,' she whispered as I drew her to my side. Whoever had lost a treasure I knew that night that I had gained one.*

In this extract, Watson opens the box that is supposed to contain the Great Agra Treasure.

Starting with this extract, explore how Conan Doyle writes about wealth and its effect
on people. Write about:

- how Conan Doyle writes about the treasure in this extract
- how Conan Doyle writes about the treasure and wealth in general in the novel as a whole. **[40 marks]**

8. **H. G. Wells: *The War of the Worlds***

Answer both parts of the question.

> **Read Book 1 Chapter 11 from**
>
> *In a few minutes there was, so far as the soldier could see, not a living thing left upon the common, and every bush and tree upon it that was not already a blackened skeleton was burning.*
>
> **to**
>
> *That was the story I got from him, bit by bit.*

In this extract the narrator relates the artilleryman's account of his experience.

a) Write about how Wells uses the artilleryman's story to explore the effects of war on civilians. Give examples from the extract to support your ideas.

b) In this chapter the narrator sees the result of the Martian attack and hears about it from a soldier. Explain how Wells writes about the experience of war **elsewhere** in the novel.

In your answer you must consider:
- how he describes war
- the effects of war.

[40 marks]

9. **George Eliot: *Silas Marner***

Answer both parts of the question.

> **Read Chapter 10 from**
>
> *And yet he was not utterly forsaken in his trouble.*
>
> **to**
>
> *'Well, Master Marner, you're no worse off nor other poor folks, after all; and if you was to be crippled, the parish 'ud give you a 'lowance.'*

In this chapter Eliot describes how the villagers' attitude to Silas Marner changes after the robbery.

a) Explore how Eliot presents the villagers of Raveloe and their attitude to Marner. Give examples from the extract to support your ideas.

b) In this extract Eliot describes the villagers' reaction to Marner's changed circumstances. Explain how the people of Raveloe treat Marner **elsewhere** in the novel.

In your answer you must consider:
- how they react to him and treat him
- what this tells us about the community.

[40 marks]

English Literature: Modern Texts

Answer one question from this section on the text you have studied.

You should spend between 45 and 55 minutes on the question.

1. **J. B. Priestley: *An Inspector Calls***

Read Act 3 from	
INSPECTOR	(*taking charge, masterfully*). Stop!
to	
INSPECTOR	And I tell you that the time will soon come when, if men will not learn that lesson, then they will be taught it in fire and blood and anguish. Good-night.

Use this extract and your knowledge of the whole play to answer this question.

Write about the role and significance of Inspector Goole and how he is presented throughout the play.

In your response you should:
* refer to the extract and the play as a whole
* show your understanding of characters and events in the play. **[40 marks]**

2. **Willy Russell: *Blood Brothers***

Read Act 1 from	
LINDA:	Leave him alone!
to	
MICKEY:	Well, my mum says I haven't got to play with you. But take no notice of mothers. They're soft. Come on, I've got Linda with me. She's a girl but she's all right.

Use this extract and your knowledge of the whole play to answer this question.

Write about the character of Linda, her relationship with Mickey and Edward, and how she is presented throughout the play.

In your response you should:
* refer to the extract and the play as a whole
* show your understanding of characters and events in the play. **[40 marks]**

3. **Alan Bennett: *The History Boys***

> **Read Act 1 from**
> MRS LINTOTT   It's a test. A way of finding out if you've ceased to be a teacher and become a friend.
> **to**
> POSNER   Yes, sir.
>   No, sir.

Use this extract and your knowledge of the whole novel to answer this question.

Write about how Bennett shows friendships between teachers and boys in the play.

In your response you should:
- refer to the extract and the novel as a whole
- show your understanding of characters and events in the novel.   **[40 marks]**

4. **Dennis Kelly: *DNA***

How does Kelly write about young people's morality (or lack of morality) in *DNA*?

Write about:
- the moral choices made by the young people in *DNA*
- how Kelly presents their moral choices in the play.   **[40 marks]**

5. **Simon Stephens: *The Curious Incident of the Dog in the Night-Time***

> **Read Part 1 from**
> CHRISTOPHER   I'm sorry.
> **to**
> ED   Yes Christopher you could say that. You could very well say that.

Use this extract and your knowledge of the whole novel to answer this question.

Write about how Christopher changes as a result of the death of Wellington.

In your response you should:
- refer to the extract and the novel as a whole
- show your understanding of characters and events in the novel.   **[40 marks]**

6. **Shelagh Delaney: *A Taste of Honey***

> **Read Act 2 from**
> JO   I don't know much about love. I've never been too familiar with it.
> **to**
> GEOF   Well, she's your mother. Do you know her address?

Use this extract and your knowledge of the whole novel to answer this question.

Write about how Delaney presents different ideas about motherhood.

In your response you should:
- refer to the extract and the novel as a whole
- show your understanding of characters and events in the novel.   **[40 marks]**

7. **William Golding: *Lord of the Flies***

   I should have thought that a pack of British boys – you're all British aren't you? – would have been able to put up a better show than that –

   To what extent is the idea of 'Britishness' important in *Lord of the Flies*? You **must** refer to the context of the novel in your answer.   [40 marks]

8. **AQA Anthology: *Telling Tales***

   How do writers explore how people change in 'The Darkness Out There' and one other story from *Telling Tales*?

   Write about:
   - how people change in the two stories
   - how the writers present these changes.   [40 marks]

9. **George Orwell: *Animal Farm***

   All that year the animals worked like slaves. But they were happy in their work; they grudged no effort or sacrifice, well aware that everything they did was for the benefit of themselves and those of their kind who would come after them, and not for a pack of idle thieving human beings.

   Explore how the pigs become more like humans as the novel progresses and how the other animals react to this. You **must** refer to the context of the novel in your answer.   [40 marks]

10. **Kazuo Ishiguro: *Never Let Me Go***

    > **Read Chapter 14 from**
    > *Ruth gave him an irritated look.*
    > **to**
    > *Look down the toilet, that's where you'll find we all came from.*

    Use this extract and your knowledge of the whole novel to answer this question.

    Write about how Ishiguro explores ideas about what it means to be human.

    In your response you should:
    - refer to the extract and the novel as a whole
    - show your understanding of characters and events in the novel.   [40 marks]

11. Meera Syal: *Anita and Me*

> **Read Chapter 2 from**
> *Whenever my father got sick of our three-up-three-down with its high uneven walls and narrow winding stairs, sick of the damp in the pantry, the outside toilet, the three buses it took to get to work, taking a bath in our bike shed and having to whisper when he wanted to shout, he'd turn to my mother and say, 'You wanted this house, remember that.'*
> **to**
> *When she stepped off the bus in Tollington, she did not see the outside lavvy or the apology for a garden or the medieval kitchen, she saw fields and trees, light and space, and a horizon that welcomed the sky which, on a warm night and through squinted eyes, could almost look something like home.*

Use this extract and your knowledge of the whole novel to answer this question.

Write about Meena's family's feelings about Tollington.

In your response you should:
* refer to the extract and the novel as a whole
* show your understanding of characters and events in the novel.   **[40 marks]**

12. Stephen Kelman: *Pigeon English*

How does Kelman present female characters in *Pigeon English*?

Write about:
* examples of female characters in *Pigeon English*
* how Kelman presents female characters.   **[40 marks]**

13. Harold Brighouse: *Hobson's Choice*

WILLIE   *I'm not ambitious that I know of.*

MAGGIE   *No. But you're going to be. I'll see to that.*

Explore how Brighouse writes about ambition and aspiration in *Hobson's Choice*.
You **must** refer to the context of the play in your answer.   **[40 marks]**

14. R.C. Sherriff: *Journey's End*

It was after I came back here – in that awful affair on Vimy Ridge. I knew I'd go mad if I didn't break the strain.

Explore how Sherriff presents the character of Stanhope in *Journey's End*.
You **must** refer to the context of the play in your answer.   **[40 marks]**

15. Charlotte Keatley: *My Mother Said I Never Should*

> **Read Act 1 Scene 7 from**
>
> | JACKIE | She has to have a red sock to go to sleep. |
> |---|---|
> | **to** | |
> | MARGARET | There now, there now, hush! Did you have a nasty dream? Mummy's here now...Mummy's here, Rosie. There now...Did you have a bad dream, Jackie? It's all right. Ssh...ssh... |

a) How does Keatley explore Jackie and Margaret's feelings about Rosie in this extract?

b) Write about how she explores tension between generations in another part of the play. **[40 marks]**

16. Susan Hill: *The Woman in Black*

This is all nonsense, fantasy, it is not like this. Nothing so blood-curdling and becreepered and crude – not so...so laughable. The truth is quite other, and altogether more terrible.

How is *The Woman in Black* made frightening? You **must** refer to the context of the novel in your answer. **[40 marks]**

17. Jeanette Winterson: *Oranges Are Not the Only Fruit*

> **Read 'Exodus' from**
>
> *Over the years I did my best to win a prize; some wish to better the world and still scorn it.*
>
> **to**
>
> *I was not a selfish child and, understanding the nature of genius, would have happily bowed to another's talent, but not to three eggs covered in cotton wool, entitled 'Easter Bunnies'.*

Use this extract and your knowledge of the whole novel to answer the question.

Oranges Are Not the Only Fruit has been called a 'Kunstlerroman', a novel about the development of an artist.

Explore how Winterson shows Jeanette's creative development.

In your response you should:
* refer to the extract and the novel as a whole
* show your understanding of characters and events in the novel. **[40 marks]**

English Literature: Poetry and Unseen Poetry

Answer the question(s) for the exam board you are studying.

AQA Anthology

You should spend between 35 and 45 minutes on this question.

EITHER

1. Compare the way poets use images of nature to convey feelings in 'Winter Swans' and one other poem from 'Love and Relationships'.　　**[20 marks]**

OR

2. Compare the way poets write about how people are changed by experience in 'Remains' and one other poem from 'Power and Conflict'.　　**[20 marks]**

Edexcel Anthology

You are advised to spend about 35 minutes on this question.

EITHER

3. Read 'My Last Duchess'. Choose one other poem from 'Relationships'. Compare how the poets explore broken or unhappy relationships in the two poems.

   In your answer you should consider:
   • the poets' use of language, form and structure
   • the influence of the contexts in which the poems were written.　　**[20 marks]**

OR

4. Read 'What Were they Like?'. Choose one other poem from 'Conflict'. Compare how the poets present victims in both poems.

   In your answer you should consider:
   • the poets' use of language, form and structure
   • the influence of the contexts in which the poems were written.　　**[20 marks]**

OR

5. Read 'On Westminster Bridge'. Choose one other poem from 'Time and Place'. Compare how the poets describe life-changing moments inspired by places.

   In your answer you should consider:
   • the poets' use of language, form and structure
   • the influence of the contexts in which the poems were written.　　**[20 marks]**

WJEC Eduqas Anthology

6. Answer both part (a) and part (b).

You are advised to spend about 20 minutes on part (a) and about 40 minutes on part (b).

a) Read Elizabeth Barrett Browning's Sonnet 43.
   In this poem Barrett Browning explores her feelings of romantic love. Write about the way she presents her feelings in this poem.

b) Choose another poem from the anthology in which the poet also writes about love. Compare the presentation of love in your chosen poem to the presentation of love in Sonnet 43.

In your answer to part (b) you should compare:
- the content and structure of the poems – what they are about and how they are organised
- how the writers create effects, using appropriate terminology where relevant
- the contexts of the poems, and how these may have influenced the ideas in them. **[20 marks]**

OCR Anthology

EITHER

7. Love and Relationships

Read 'Bright Star' and 'The Darkling Thrush' (on page 58) and then answer both parts of the question.
a) Compare how the poets use images from nature to explore their own feelings. **[20 marks]**
b) Explore in detail how one other poem from the anthology uses nature to express feelings. **[20 marks]**

OR

8. Conflict

Read 'Boat Stealing' (from *The Prelude*) and 'The Darkling Thrush' (on page 58) and then answer both parts of the question.
a) Compare how the poems present a spiritual experience. **[20 marks]**
b) Explore in detail one other poem from the anthology which presents an experience that has a profound effect. **[20 marks]**

OR

9. Youth and Age

Read 'Farther' and 'The Darkling Thrush' (on page 58) and then answer both parts of the question.
a) Compare how the poets write about landscapes and the feelings they inspire in the poets. **[20 marks]**
b) Explore in detail one other poem from the anthology that uses place to present the poet's feelings. **[20 marks]**

Unseen Poetry

Answer both questions.

You should spend a total of between 40 and 50 minutes on both questions.

1. Read 'The Darkling Thrush' by Thomas Hardy.

The Darkling Thrush

I leant upon a coppice gate
      When Frost was spectre-gray,
And Winter's dregs made desolate
      The weakening eye of day.
The tangled bine-stems scored the sky
      Like strings of broken lyres,
And all mankind that haunted nigh
      Had sought their household fires.

The land's sharp features seemed to me
      The Century's corpse outleant,
Its crypt the cloudy canopy,
      The wind its death-lament.
The ancient pulse of germ and birth
      Was shrunken hard and dry,
And every spirit upon earth
      Seemed fervourless as I.

At once a voice arose among
      The bleak twigs overhead
In a full-hearted evensong
      Of joy illimited;
An aged thrush, frail, gaunt and small,
      With blast-beruffled plume,
Had chosen thus to fling his soul
      Upon the growing gloom.

So little cause for carolings
      Of such ecstatic sound
Was written on terrestrial things
      Afar or nigh around,
That I could think there trembled through
      His happy goodnight air
Some blessed Hope, whereof he knew,
      And I was unaware.

                    Thomas Hardy

a) In 'The Darkling Thrush' how does the poet use natural imagery to present his mood and feelings?

b) Now read 'Spellbound' by Emily Jane Brontë.

Spellbound

The night is darkening round me,
The wild winds coldly blow;
But a tyrant spell has bound me
And I cannot, cannot go.

The giant trees are bending
Their bare boughs weighed with snow.
And the storm is fast descending,
And yet I cannot go.

Clouds beyond clouds above me,
Wastes beyond wastes below;
But nothing drear can move me;
I will not, cannot go.

Emily Jane Brontë

In both 'The Darkling Thrush' and 'Spellbound' the poets write about nature and their own feelings.

What are the similarities and/or differences between the ways the poets present nature and their feelings?

[20 marks]

END OF QUESTIONS

*For answers worth 8 marks or more, detailed mark schemes are given which include the skills shown in your answer, and examples of content you might have included. **They are not full or model answers.** Look at the mark schemes and decide which description is closest to your answer. The number of marks and approximate grade are given.*

English Language Set A

Pages 4–7: Reading Literary Texts and Creative Writing

1. I'd like to see Ireland **again;** The people at **home. [1 mark for each up to a maximum of 2]**
2. **a) Duncannon [1] b) Five miles [1]**
3. **[Maximum 8 marks]**

Marks	Skills	Example of Possible Content
7–8 (Grade 7–9)	You have: analysed the effects of the choice of structural features and language; used an appropriate range of quotations; used sophisticated subject terminology appropriately.	In the first paragraph, the reported speech quickly establishes the protagonist's situation, as well as the American location of the story ('a slum in the Bowery… Central Park'). However, the following two lines of direct speech between the protagonist and the doctor, and the doctor's suggestion that the (so far unnamed) protagonist should go to Ireland from where he will return a 'new man', lead us to the inciting incident: his decision to go 'home'. Within two lines we are transported from New York to Cork, the sudden change of place suggesting that there will indeed be as great and sudden a change in the protagonist.
5–6 (Grade 4–6)	You have: clearly explained the effects of structural features and language; used a range of relevant quotations; used subject terminology appropriately.	The story opens in New York but within a few lines the protagonist is in Ireland. The description of the bar contrasts with later descriptions of Ireland. The writer does not tell us much about the man, not even his name (he uses the third person pronoun 'he') or what is wrong with his health, though the title and the doctor's prescription of 'a sea voyage' suggest it might just be homesickness. This lack of information would intrigue the reader. Who is he? Will he recover? What will he find in Ireland and will he 'come back a new man'?
3–4 (Grade 2–3)	You have: commented on the effect of language and/or structure; used some relevant quotations; used some subject terminology, not always appropriately.	The writer starts by describing the man in New York. He does not say what is wrong with him but the doctor says 'a sea voyage is what you want' so it does not sound serious. The language is plain and does not give away the man's thoughts: 'the doctor was right'. We might find out if this is true.
1–2 (Grade U–1)	You have: tried to comment on the effect of language and/or structure; referred to the text; mentioned subject terminology.	He goes to the doctor's. In their conversation he tells him to go to Ireland. We wonder what will happen next.

4. **[Maximum 8 marks]**

Marks	Skills	Example of Possible Content
7–8 (Grade 7–9)	You have: analysed the use of language; chosen an appropriate range of examples; used a range of subject terminology accurately.	The writer describes Duncannon through the lens of the protagonist's memories. What is described is not what Bryden sees now (he has not yet arrived at Duncannon) but what he 'could see' in his mind's eye. He starts with a topographical explanation of the village's location 'among the rocks of the large headland' before listing its features without the embellishment of adverbs or figurative imagery. He then moves on to a list of the villagers' activities, using a series of present participles and ending with a particular memory, made more vivid by the use of a name and a direct object: 'Michael Malia building a wall'.

Marks	Skills	Example of Possible Content
5–6 (Grade 4–6)	You have: clearly explained the effect of language choices; chosen relevant examples; used subject terminology accurately.	The writer starts by giving us information, in a very straightforward way, about where the village is and describes the peaceful surroundings of the lake. Then he gives a list of what is in the village. Mentioning the 'Georgian mansion' makes him think of the people who lived there. He makes everyone sound friendly – they were 'boys together' – and hard-working, using verbs like 'mowing, reaping, digging'. He moves from describing a general scene to one person.
3–4 (Grade 2–3)	You have: tried to comment on the effect of language; chosen some relevant examples; used some subject terminology, not always accurately.	He gives a list of what he can see: 'the houses and the streets and the fields'. He talks about all the jobs that the 'villagers' used to do in the past and it is 'as clear as if it were yesterday' to him.
1–2 (Grade U–1)	You have: commented in a simple way on language; given simple examples; mentioned subject terminology.	He describes the village using words like 'houses' and 'fields'.

5. [Maximum 20 marks]

Marks	Skills	Example of Possible Content
16–20 (Grade 7–9)	You have: critically evaluated the text in a detailed way; used examples from the text to explain your views convincingly; analysed a range of writer's methods; used a range of relevant quotations to support your views.	The writer tells us very little about Bryden's appearance: when he finally meets Mike Scully we are told of his 'great width of chest' and 'sallow' complexion, giving mixed messages about his health. He says nothing directly about his character. From the first few lines we can infer some facts about him: that he lives in New York, that he is a barman, that he is not well and that he comes originally from Ireland. This is all we need to know about him before he leaves New York. Perhaps the most important thing about him is that he is going 'home'; he could be an archetype of any emigrant from Europe to America. It is a third person narrative but the story is mostly told from Bryden's point of view. He shares his memories of his 'native village', building a picture of his background and giving the impression of a man who remembers the past with affection, 'all as clear as if it were yesterday'. He also looks to the future, the story of Mike Scully's house inspiring a 'reverie' about what he himself might achieve.
11–15 (Grade 4–6)	You have: clearly evaluated the text; used examples from the text to explain your views clearly; clearly explained the effect of the writer's methods; used relevant quotations to support your views.	At the beginning we find out that he works as a barman in a poor part of New York: 'the bar-room was a slum in the Bowery'. We also know he is not well as he visits the doctor, but there is no detail about his illness and maybe he is just homesick. The way he thinks about the old days suggests he is nostalgic for the days 'before he went to America'. Mike gives us an ambiguous message. He is a 'fine man', referring to his 'great width of chest', so he must be strong. However, he also says he is 'very sallow in the cheeks' which suggests that he is not healthy.
6–10 (Grade 2–3)	You have: tried to comment on the text; given an example from the text to explain your views; tried to comment on the writer's methods; used some quotations, which sometimes support your views.	At first I get the impression that he is sick and not very happy in New York. He must work hard and not have much fun. He remembers a different life in Ireland 'as if it was yesterday'. The writer describes his thoughts about his home and the people he knew. Mike calls him 'a fine man' so he must be strong even though he is 'thin in the cheeks'.

1–5 (Grade U–1)	You have: made simple comments on the text; given a simple example from the text; mentioned the writer's methods; referred to the text.	He is sick and he lives in the Bowery but he goes back to Ireland. The writer tells us this. He seems pleased to be back at 'home'.

6. (a) and (b) [Maximum 40]
Content and Organisation [Maximum 24]:

22–24 marks (Grade 8–9)	**Content:** You have communicated convincingly and compellingly throughout; your tone, style and register assuredly match purpose, form and audience; you have used an extensive and ambitious vocabulary with sustained crafting of linguistic devices. **Organisation:** Your writing is highly structured and developed, including a range of integrated and complex ideas; your paragraphs are fluently linked with integrated discourse markers; you have used a variety of structural features in an inventive way.
19–21 marks (Grade 6–7)	**Content:** You have communicated convincingly; your tone, style and register consistently match purpose, form and audience; you have used an extensive vocabulary with evidence of conscious crafting of linguistic devices. **Organisation:** Your writing is structured and developed, including a range of engaging complex ideas; you have used paragraphs consistently with integrated discourse markers; you have used a variety of structural features effectively.
16–18 marks (Grade 5)	**Content:** You have communicated clearly and effectively; your tone, style and register match purpose, form and audience; you have used an increasingly sophisticated vocabulary with a range of appropriate linguistic devices. **Organisation:** Your writing is engaging, including a range of engaging, detailed, connected ideas; you have used paragraphs coherently with integrated discourse markers; you have used structural features effectively.
13–15 marks (Grade 4)	**Content:** You have communicated clearly; your tone, style and register generally match purpose, form and audience; you have used vocabulary for effect with a range of linguistic devices. **Organisation:** Your writing is engaging, including a range of connected ideas; you have usually used paragraphs coherently with a range of discourse markers; you have usually used structural features effectively.
10–12 marks (Grade 3)	**Content:** You have communicated mostly successfully; you have tried to match tone, style and register to purpose, form and audience; you have used vocabulary consciously and used some linguistic devices. **Organisation:** Your writing includes linked and relevant ideas; you have sometimes used paragraphs and discourse markers; you have used some structural features.
7–9 marks (Grade 2)	**Content:** You have communicated with some success; you have tried to match register to purpose, form and audience; you have begun to vary vocabulary and used some linguistic devices. **Organisation:** Your writing includes some linked and relevant ideas; you have tried to write in paragraphs with some discourse markers, not always successfully; you have tried to use structural features.
4–6 marks (Grade 1)	**Content:** You have communicated your ideas; you have shown a simple awareness of purpose, form and audience; you have used a simple vocabulary and simple linguistic devices. **Organisation:** Your writing includes one or two relevant ideas, simply linked; you have tried to write in paragraphs, but the result is random; you have tried to use simple structural features.
1–3 marks (Grade U)	**Content:** You have communicated some meaning; you have shown an occasional sense of purpose, form and audience; you have used a simple vocabulary. **Organisation:** Your writing includes one or two unlinked ideas; you have not written in paragraphs; you may have tried to use simple structural features.

Technical Accuracy [Maximum 16]:

13–16 marks (Grade 7–9)	You have: consistently demarcated sentences accurately; used a wide range of punctuation with a high level of accuracy; used a full range of sentence forms for effect; used Standard English consistently and accurately with secure control of grammatical structures; achieved a high level of accuracy in spelling, including ambitious vocabulary and your use of vocabulary is extensive and sophisticated.
9–12 marks (Grade 4–6)	You have: usually demarcated sentences accurately; used a range of punctuation, usually accurately; used a variety of sentence forms for effect; used Standard English appropriately with control of grammatical structures; spelled most words, including complex and irregular words, correctly and your use of vocabulary is increasingly sophisticated.
5–8 marks (Grade 2–3)	You have: usually demarcated sentences securely; used a range of punctuation sometimes accurately; tried to use a variety of sentence forms; used some Standard English with some control of agreement; spelled some complex and irregular words correctly; used a varied vocabulary.
1–4 marks (Grade U-1)	You have: occasionally demarcated sentences; used some punctuation; used a simple range of sentence forms; occasionally used Standard English with limited control of agreement; spelled basic words correctly; used a simple vocabulary.

(a) There are many possible responses. Here is an example of part of a possible answer:

Suddenly a massive edifice of stone appears through the mist. A landscape that seemed deserted as we rowed steadily, carefully, unseeing across the lough – the only sound the regular splish-splash of our innocent oars – is now dominated by this ancient fortress. It is beautiful, but its beauty is cold and forbidding. How long has it stood sentinel over these dark waters? How long has it stood proud among the rolling hills, a symbol of man's power? How long has it stood witness to the ebb and flow of human history?

(b) There are many possible responses. Here is an example of part of a possible answer:

I sat on the park bench and thought about what the doctor had said. Good news. I should have been elated. I could have celebrated: leapt for joy; turned cartwheels; fallen to the ground and sobbed for joy. But I felt nothing. Well, not exactly nothing. I felt (and I don't know how to put this without causing offence) disappointed. I knew this was not how I should be feeling and I resisted it – at first. But it came like a great wave and knocked me off my feet. Then came another wave, a darker, more sinister wave. A new feeling overwhelmed me and I let myself drown in it. It was fear.

Pages 8–12: Reading Non-fiction and Non-fiction/Transactional Writing

1. A D F G. **[Maximum 4 – if more than 4 boxes are shaded 0 marks should be given]**
2. **[Maximum 8]**

Marks	Skills	Example of Possible Content
7–8 (Grade 7–9)	You have: given a perceptive interpretation of both texts; synthesised evidence from the texts; used appropriate quotations from both texts.	Both Lucy's mill and Archie's bakery are praised by the writers but are very different places. Lucy's is highly mechanised and is 'one of the largest' mills in Birmingham, producing ten times the amount of bread that Archie's produces. Archie's 'real bread' methods of doing everything by hand might be a reaction to firms like Lucy's. The bread itself is basically the same, made of 'flour, and water, and yeast, and salt'. However, Archie produces a variety of 'the finest artisan breads' whereas the article about Lucy's does not mention any variety. The only other thing they sell is flour, while Archie's also has cakes and pastries. Lucy's does not sell direct to people but delivers to 'hucksters' shops'. Archie's is a single shop that people come to but they do deliver locally.
5–6 (Grade 4–6)	You have: started to interpret both texts; shown clear connections between texts; used relevant quotations from both texts.	Lucy's is a huge bread mill, 'one of the largest' in Birmingham, making 2000 loaves a day but Archie's is 'a village bakery' making about 200. He makes his bread 'by hand' but Lucy's uses machines powered by steam. Lucy's sells flour and bread to shops, while Archie sells bread and 'fabulous choux pastry' in his own shop.

Answers

3–4 (Grade 2–4)	You have: tried to infer from one/both texts; tried to link evidence between texts; used some quotations from both texts.	Lucy's is one of six 'large bread mills' in Birmingham. Everything is done using 'steam'. Archie does not use machines – 'it's all done by hand'. Lucy's makes a lot more bread than Archie's.
1–2 (Grade U-1)	You have: paraphrased texts but have not inferred; made simple or no links between texts; referred to one/both texts.	The first one says there is a new mill in Birmingham. The second is about Archie's artisan bread.

3. [Maximum 12]

Marks	Skills	Example of Possible Content
10–12 (Grade 7–9)	You have: analysed the effects of the choice of language; used an appropriate range of quotations; used sophisticated subject terminology appropriately.	The writer tries to engage readers by using informal language ('Hi') and personalising his business, using first and second person pronouns constantly to involve us, as well as repeating his and his wife's names. This could be seen as being friendly (first name terms) but also establishes the couple as a 'brand'. Fabienne's name is shortened to 'Fab', as is the word 'fabulous', contributing to the relentlessly positive (almost boastful) feeling of the piece. Archie's aim is to appear like one of us ('local lad') but also superior because of his experience, training in Paris with 'artisan bakers' and his skills: he is a 'master baker'. This is reinforced by the specialised language he uses: 'fermentation … kneading'. In contrast with his insistence on being 'local' he likes to show off the French connection, using words like 'boulangerie'.
7–9 (Grade 4–6)	You have: clearly explained the effects of the choice of language; used a range of relevant quotations; used subject terminology appropriately.	The tone is quite informal and friendly. The first part is very personal with repetition of the first person pronouns 'I' and 'we' making us think Archie is talking to us personally. Then he explains things in detail and uses technical terms like 'sourdough' to impress us with his expertise. He also uses French words like 'patissiere', maybe because his wife is French but maybe because snobbish people like French things and think they're better. He keeps repeating words like 'local' and 'artisan' to get the message across that he is special.
4–6 (Grade 2–3)	You have: tried to comment on the effect of language; used some relevant quotations; used some subject terminology, not always appropriately.	It is informal and he writes as if he wants to know you, using pronouns 'I' and 'we' and giving a list of what he and his wife have done. He says technical things about the bread, using words like 'starter' and 'sourdough' so you know he's an expert.
1–3 (Grade U-1)	You have: commented on the effect of language; referred to text; mentioned subject terminology.	The language is friendly. He says 'Hi' and uses words like 'I' and 'we'.

Answers

4. [Maximum 16]

Marks	Skills	Example of Possible Content
13–16 (Grade 7–9)	You have: compared ideas and perspectives in a perceptive way; analysed methods used to convey ideas and perspectives; used a range of appropriate quotations.	The two sources have different purposes. Dodd wants his readers to understand how bread is made and how the manufacturers could improve production. His piece is like an academic paper, quoting a French report on the industry and describing processes in London, Paris and Birmingham. Archie also explains bread-making but he wants to drum up business for his own small bakery. He thinks on a much smaller scale. Some of the terminology is similar and both obviously understand the subject. They both use the words 'mix/mixing' and 'knead/kneading' and describe the same basic ingredients. However, they have opposite points of view on mechanising the bread-making process. To Dodd the traditional way of bread-making he has observed is 'rude and primitive', making the 'uncouthness' of the bakers seem revolting and unhygienic. To him steam mills and other machines can only be an improvement. Archie, writing over 150 years later, says he 'bakes… with the heart' and, by using terms like 'real bread', implies that there is something false and unhealthy about bread produced in factories.
9–12 (Grade 4–6)	You have: compared ideas and perspectives in a clear and relevant way; explained clearly methods used to convey ideas and perspectives; used relevant quotations from both texts.	Source A is about the way bread is made in the 1850s and looks at how it can be improved. The writer thinks making bread by hand is inefficient. He uses words like 'clumsiness', 'straddling and wriggling' and 'uncouthness' which all make it seem unpleasant. In contrast, the big steam mills in Birmingham seem much better. Source B, however, rejects 'white sliced pre-packaged bread' and wants to go back to doing everything by hand. He paints a picture of everything being done properly in a nice family environment. He is not interested in producing huge amounts of bread.
5–8 (Grade 2–3)	You have: identified some differences between ideas and perspectives; commented on methods used to convey ideas and perspectives; used some quotations from one or both texts.	Dodd explains in detail how bread is made in Paris. He does not think it should be done like this but would like them to use machines. This is 'progress' and he gives examples of big mills in Birmingham where they use machines and make 2000 loaves a day. Archie is the opposite. He is proud of making a small amount of bread 'by hand'. He calls it 'real bread' and explains what goes into it and who makes it.
1–4 (Grade U-1)	You have: referred to different ideas and perspectives; identified how differences are conveyed; made simple references to one or both texts.	The first writer says bread-making is very hard work but he thinks it could be easier with machines. Archie does not like machines – 'it's all done by hand'.

5. Look at the mark scheme for question 6 on pages 62–63. This task is marked for content and organisation, and for technical accuracy. **[Maximum 40]**

There are many possible responses. Here is an example of part of a possible answer:

Recently, I watched a programme on television about British families' eating habits. It was primarily concerned with budgeting but also looked at nutrition and healthy eating. On it a young woman, the mother of the family, declared (in all seriousness) that she bought expensive, processed cheese slices because it takes so long to slice cheese! I accept that she led a busy life, with a full-time job, two children and a house to look after, but surely nobody is too busy to slice cheese.

This was just one of many examples of people wasting money on often unhealthy processed foods when fresh produce, bought more cheaply and prepared at home – as the woman in question discovered – is not only better for us physically but can also help to give us a better quality of family life. How? Far from being a waste of time, cooking can be relaxing and enjoyable. It is also something families can do together, bringing them closer as they work towards a shared goal.

English Language Set B

Pages 14–17: Reading Literary Texts and Creative Writing

1. **Any four from:** the open square; the tops of the trees; a peddler; someone singing; sparrows; patches of blue sky
   [1 mark for each up to a maximum of 4]
2. **[Maximum 8 marks]**

Marks	Skills	Example of Possible Content
7–8 (Grade 7–9)	You have: analysed the effects of the choice of language; used an appropriate range of quotations; used sophisticated subject terminology appropriately.	The omniscient narrator, describing Louise's appearance and her personality, uses language that suggests a lack of passion. She is 'calm' and has a 'dull stare' with her look indicating 'a suspension of intelligent thought'. From this, the reader might think she was stunned by her news or just unfeeling but the references to 'repression' and 'a certain strength' alert us to something going on under the surface. Chopin uses an extended metaphor to convey how she discovers her true feelings. They could be a monster 'creeping … reaching', the present participles here giving a sense of movement and danger. Her reaction is expressed using the kind of violent vocabulary one might expect in a horror story. 'Her bosom rose and fell tumultuously' suggests she is being physically attacked and the use of the verb 'to possess' could suggest rape, as does the feminine powerlessness of her 'white slender hands', which provide a simile for her weak 'will'.
5–6 (Grade 4–6)	You have: clearly explained the effects of language; used a range of relevant quotations; used subject terminology appropriately.	At first words like 'calm', 'dull' and 'gaze' suggest that she is not really upset about her husband's death and is perhaps a bit stupid. But then her feelings change and there are a lot of violent words like the adverb 'tumultuously' and the phrase 'beating it back'. We do not know what she is fighting but by using the imagery of something attacking Louise, Chopin conveys how frightened she is and how much this 'creeping' feeling could affect her.
3–4 (Grade 2–3)	You have: commented on the effect of language; used some relevant quotations; used some subject terminology, not always appropriately.	She seems not to be feeling much because she has a 'dull stare'. She thinks something frightening is going to happen, using metaphors as if it is an animal 'creeping'.
1–2 (Grade U-1)	You have: tried to comment on the effect of language; referred to the text; mentioned subject terminology.	She was young and she was afraid. The writer uses the word 'fearfully' to describe her.

3. [Maximum 8 marks]

Marks	Skills	Example of Possible Content
7–8 (Grade 7–9)	You have: analysed the use of structural features; chosen an appropriate range of examples; used a range of subject terminology accurately.	The writer quickly introduces the situation and characters, briefly alluding to Louise's health. Brently's death is a shocking event. The reader would expect the story to focus on Louise's reaction and how she might cope. As the focus shifts to Louise, alone in her room, the writer explores her feelings and there is a turning point when she and the reader realise that her life will change but not in the way they might have expected. The mood changes with the protagonist's mood to one of hope and expectation. The next turning point, the unexpected entrance of Louise's husband, is shocking and dashes all her hopes. It seems like the end but Chopin plays a trick on the reader. The story is not really over. The reader might have forgotten the opening sentence about Louise's 'heart trouble' but now it creates the 'sting in the tail' with the short penultimate sentence – 'But Richards was too late' – stunning the reader before the final sentence economically explains what has happened and leaves us with an ambiguous and ironic sentiment.
5–6 (Grade 4–6)	You have: clearly explained the effect of structural features; chosen relevant examples; used subject terminology accurately.	The story starts with Louise hearing the news of her husband's death. The focus is on how people break the news to her and how it has happened before switching to Louise's reaction, which is not 'as many other women' would have reacted but still quite normal. Then the writer describes Louise alone in her room and how her reaction changes from being stunned to a violent one of being glad she is 'free'. This is a turning point and the writer tells us how her life might be and seems to be a happy ending for her but then there is a shocking twist when her husband walks in. Ironically, it is Louise who ends up dead.
3–4 (Grade 2–3)	You have: tried to comment on structure; chosen some relevant examples; used some subject terminology, not always accurately.	At the beginning Louise hears about her husband's death. The first surprise is that she 'did not hear the story as many women have'. We wonder what her reaction will be. At first she is 'dull' but then she is glad: 'Free, free, free!' But this is not the last surprise. The twist at the end is that he is not dead and she dies when she hears the news.
1–2 (Grade U-1)	You have: commented in a simple way on structure; given simple examples; mentioned subject terminology.	At the start she thinks he is dead. At the end she finds out he isn't and she dies.

4. [Maximum 20 marks]

Marks	Skills	Example of Possible Content
16–20 (Grade 7–9)	You have: critically evaluated the text in a detailed way; used examples from the text to explain your views convincingly; analysed a range of writer's methods; used a range of relevant quotations to support your views.	Louise is introduced as someone to be taken care of, told bad news in 'veiled hints', the implication being that she is emotionally, as well as physically, fragile. Her first reaction to the news does nothing to dispel this, the 'wild abandonment' suggesting hysteria. This makes what follows all the more surprising. Chopin describes her physically, the 'calm' of her face reflecting her mood. We also learn about her 'strength' and the word 'repression' is used, suggesting this is not the woman we thought she was. Her excitement and fear about the 'something coming to her' indicate a massive shift in her life, which could be good or bad, but when she cries 'Free, free, free' we know that she must see marriage as a prison from which she is about to be liberated. Louise is clearly dependent on her husband and limited in her choices as a wife. However, Chopin speaks of 'men and women' imposing their 'will upon a fellow creature', suggesting she sees marriage as prison for both sexes.
11–15 (Grade 4–6)	You have: clearly evaluated the text; used examples from the text to explain your views clearly; clearly explained the effect of the writer's methods; used some relevant quotations to support your views.	Louise's friends and family are protective of her because of her weak health and because of her husband's 'death' but she is not really a weak character. She has 'a certain strength'. The writer also mentions 'repression' so we feel she does not usually let out her feelings. These feelings change. The description of her 'wild abandonment' followed by her 'calm' could be normal stages in grief. She must see marriage as a prison as she shouts 'Free, free, free!' Through her the writer explores ideas about women and marriage. She does not look forward to life alone because her marriage is bad – she had loved him – but 'self-assertion' is more important.
6–10 (Grade 2–3)	You have: tried to comment on the text; given an example from the text to explain your views; tried to comment on the writer's methods; used some quotations, which sometimes support your views.	The writer describes her as having heart trouble, so we think she is quite delicate. When she weeps she seems sensitive and as if she loved her husband. The writer tells us what she is feeling and that she is frightened of something 'creeping out of the sky' so it is strange that she turns out to be happy about his death. She must think of marriage as a bad thing for women. She wants to 'live for herself'.
1–5 (Grade U-1)	You have: made simple comments on the text; given a simple example from the text; mentioned the writer's methods; referred to the text.	She is not like 'other women'. She is shocked at first but then she shouts out that she is 'free'. She is glad he is dead.

5. (a), (b), (c), (d) Look at the mark scheme for question 6 on pages 62–63. This task is marked for content and organisation, and for technical accuracy. **[Maximum 40]**

(a) There are many possible responses. Here is an example of part of a possible answer:

'I think you'd better sit down,' she said. 'I've got some bad news.'

The laughter stopped immediately. We all looked at her. Amy's face betrayed no emotion. Not a flicker of the eyelids. Not a quiver of the lip. She stood, straight-backed and steady, her face immobile as if carved in stone. Sphinx-like. I remembered something Gran had once said about still waters running deep. It made me impatient with Amy and her unnatural calmness.

'Okay, Amy. You've got our attention. Just say what you've got to say and go.'

(b) There are many possible responses. Here is an example of part of a possible answer:

And that was it. They were gone. 'Without a backward glance'. Why did that phrase force its way into his mind? Ridiculous. Why should they have glanced back at him? What did he want? Gratitude? Another thought – a memory of childhood – came unbidden. He was sitting on a bench – no, a pew. It was a pew because it was in the chapel. Squirming restlessly, wanting his own freedom then, he heard the reader ask, 'Were there not ten cleansed? But where are the other nine?' Only one of the cured had returned to give thanks to the Lord. Perhaps one would return for him too.

(c) There are many possible responses. Here is an example of part of a possible answer:

When she saw the story on the six o'clock news she knew instantly. She wouldn't be able to say how she knew. When, days later, she told Stephen he called it a mother's instinct but she had never believed in such things: instinct, ESP, second sight. To sensible, rational mother-of-three Rhona Chapman such things belonged in fairy stories, not in the real world, the world in which she had brought up her children. How had this tragedy – this horror – this nightmare – dared to invade her world?

(d) There are many possible responses. Here is an example of part of a possible answer:

Somebody's just come out of the flats across the street. I can just see two heads bobbing about above the cars. They're moving very quickly. The lights on the white van have just flashed on and one of them has come round to the passenger side. It's a man of about fifty, carrying a box of some sort. He's wearing overalls. They must have been doing a job in the flats. And they're gone.

Now the only movement is the pampas grass swaying slightly in the breeze. Bits of it – leaves, a stalk or two – lie on the grass before it. They must have broken off in last night's storm and now the remaining stalks lean and nod towards them, helplessly mourning their fate. Unseen, somewhere among the neatly trimmed bushes, a cat cries.

Pages 18–21: Reading Non-fiction and Non-fiction/Transactional Writing

1. B C F G. **[Maximum 4 – if more than 4 boxes are shaded 0 marks should be given]**
2. **[Maximum 8]**

Marks	Skills	Example of Possible Content
7–8 (Grade 7–9)	You have: given a perceptive interpretation of both texts; synthesised evidence from the texts; used appropriate quotations from both texts.	Both writers describe behaviour they consider to be 'familiarity' (Trollope) or 'over-familiarity' (Boyle). The former criticises the behaviour of a particular neighbour before talking about Americans in general, while the latter mentions waiters, TV presenters and teachers. Trollope acknowledges the woman is helpful and intends to be friendly, and concludes her 'violent intimacy' is the norm in the USA. Boyle does not think the behaviour he describes is genuine and thinks it is copied from an idea of American friendliness. Both are concerned with forms of address. Trollope says that she and her husband are called 'the old man' and 'the English old woman' while ordinary working people such as 'draymen, butcher's boys and labourers' are referred to as ladies and gentlemen. Boyle is concerned with service rather than class and says people in 'service industries' in France and Italy behave properly in contrast with those serving in Britain.
5–6 (Grade 4–6)	You have: started to interpret both texts; shown clear connections between texts; used relevant quotations from both texts.	Trollope writes about the manners of Americans, Boyle about British people who imitate American manners. The behaviour Trollope describes is mostly from a woman who is over friendly, using first names and calling the children 'honey'. Boyle writes mostly about waiters. He says they now say 'You guys' instead of 'Sir/Madam'. He says others, like teachers, do the same thing.
3–4 (Grade 2–4)	You have: tried to infer from one/both texts; tried to link evidence between texts; used some quotations from both texts.	The first is about a neighbour in America who is trying to be friendly. She is 'jovial' and tries to help. The waiters Boyle writes about are also meant to help but they are paid for it and might not really be friendly. They both lack respect.
1–2 (Grade U-1)	You have: paraphrased texts but have not inferred; made simple or no links between texts; referred to one/both texts.	They both talk about Americans. In the first one she meets a neighbour she does not like. The second is about waiters being rude.

3. [Maximum 12]

Marks	Skills	Example of Possible Content
10–12 (Grade 7–9)	You have: analysed the effects of the choice of language; used an appropriate range of quotations; used sophisticated subject terminology appropriately.	Trollope starts with an anecdote to illustrate her point. She describes the situation in an understated, undramatic way ('absent rather longer than we expected') so it is clear that the search is not in itself the point of the story. Her later use of hyperbole, for example 'exceedingly coarse and vehement' and 'violent intimacy', and the idea that the woman 'almost frightened' her (when you might think she'd be more frightened about her children being missing) suggests she wants to both shock and amuse, as does her reference to the 'amusement' of her children. In the second paragraph she uses a lot of direct speech to give the reader a flavour of American manners. She quotes the dialect of the Americans: 'That there lady… what is making dip-candles'. Here both the juxtaposition of the term 'lady' (in England usually someone who did not work) and 'making dip-candles' and the use of the non-standard 'that there' and 'what is' add both to the vividness of the picture and its humorous tone. Yet the tone seems affectionate, with a hint of self-deprecation, so you do not feel that she is 'making fun' of her neighbours.
7–9 (Grade 4–6)	You have: clearly explained the effects of the choice of language; used a range of relevant quotations; used subject terminology appropriately.	The narrative is formal, with long sentences and formal, old-fashioned standard English: 'our party determined' and 'such a pair had been seen to pass'. When she meets the woman whom she compares to a market woman to give readers an idea of her appearance, her language becomes more dramatic. The woman is 'coarse and vehement' and Trollope does not like her 'violent intimacy'. She wants to put across how Americans speak so she uses a lot of quotations in the second half. Phrases like 'them gentlemen' and 'that there lady' convey both their dialect and their attitude.
4–6 (Grade 2–3)	You have: tried to comment on the effect of language; used some relevant quotations; used some subject terminology, not always appropriately.	She tells the story of looking for her children in long sentences but without much description. The tone is calm so she cannot be panicking: 'They were absent rather longer than usual'. She quotes a lot of speech from Americans and writes it in a sort of dialect to make it amusing to readers: 'That there lady.'
1–3 (Grade U-1)	You have: commented on the effect of language; referred to the text; mentioned subject terminology.	She describes people and gives examples of their speech. They speak in an American way.

4. [Maximum 16]

Marks	Skills	Example of Possible Content
13–16 (Grade 7–9)	You have: compared ideas and perspectives in a perceptive way; analysed methods used to convey ideas and perspectives; used a range of appropriate quotations.	The two writers have broadly similar attitudes to manners. They both prefer a degree of formality. Trollope uses the word 'familiarity' and Boyle 'over familiarity' in the same pejorative way. Trollope is shocked ('almost frightened') by some of the ways of Americans while Boyle is 'outraged' by being addressed in a familiar, American-style way by a waiter. However, Trollope's purpose in writing is to inform her audience of the ways of Americans, remarking that such manners are 'universal' in the USA, while Boyle assumes his audience is familiar with the behaviour he is complaining about. He is putting forward an argument about the Americanisation of manners in Britain and expressing his distaste. Consequently, his tone is one of comic exaggerated outrage ('I would never leave the house'; 'never, ever') mixed with a serious attempt to analyse what he sees. Trollope too uses comedy but she is concerned more with reporting what she sees than analysis.

Answers

9–12 (Grade 4–6)	You have: compared ideas and perspectives in a clear and relevant way; explained clearly methods used to convey ideas and perspectives; used relevant quotations from both texts.	The two writers both dislike 'familiarity' and get upset by people being too informal with them. However, in Boyle's case he is only talking about people in 'service industries', while Trollope is talking about Americans in general. Trollope is writing a book about the 'manners' of Americans so we can infer that at that time people in England behaved in a very different way. Boyle's main complaint is that phrases like 'you guys' have been 'imported from America'. He wants us to be different from them. They both use quotations in order to criticise them, and amuse the reader: 'them gentlemen' and 'Listen up guys'. Boyle is angrier than Trollope, who is just surprised by what she hears.
5–8 (Grade 2–3)	You have: identified some differences between ideas and perspectives; commented on methods used to convey ideas and perspectives; used some quotations from one or both texts.	They do not like 'over familiarity' and are both bothered about how people talk to them. However, Trollope is talking about the difference between the English and Americans, while Boyle is angry about English people imitating Americans. They both try to use humour, Trollope by using language like 'violent intimacy' and describing her 'dread' of meeting the woman and Boyle by using words like 'touch their forelocks'. Both are a bit snobbish.
1–4 (Grade U-1)	You have: referred to different ideas and perspectives; identified how differences are conveyed; made simple references to one or both texts.	They both want people to be more polite and they don't like them being friendly. Trollope doesn't like Americans and Boyle doesn't like waiters.

5. Look at the mark scheme for question 6 on pages 62–63. This task is marked for content and organisation, and for technical accuracy. **[Maximum 40]**
   There are many possible responses. Here is an example of part of a possible answer:
   While it is obvious that no-one can share the same degree of intimacy with all their five hundred Facebook friends, neither can we be equally close to everyone that we know in the 'real' world. The difference surely is in the terminology, not the fact. People we refer to as 'friends' online are not friends in the traditional sense. We call them that because that is what the company that provides our means of communication calls them. They call them that because it sounds warm, positive and, well, friendly. Many of these people are really just acquaintances or contacts. They are the internet equivalent of the neighbour we nod to in the street or the girl we occasionally sit next to in French. However, that does not stop some of them becoming as close as the friends we have grown up with: sharing experiences and secrets; arguing and making up; laughing and crying together.

English Literature Set A

Pages 24–27: Shakespeare

For all questions, look at the mark scheme below. **[Maximum 40 marks]**

Marks	Skills
34–40 (Grade 8–9)	You have: responded to the task in an exploratory and critical way; used precise, appropriate references to support your interpretation; analysed the writer's methods using subject terminology appropriately; explored the effects of the writer's methods; explored links between text and ideas/context.
28–33 (Grade 6–7)	You have: responded to the task in a thoughtful, developed way; used appropriate references to support your interpretation; examined the writer's methods using subject terminology effectively; examined the effects of the writer's methods; thoughtfully considered links between text and ideas/context.
21–27 (Grade 4–5)	You have: responded to the task in a clear way; used references effectively to support your explanation; clearly explained the writer's methods using relevant subject terminology; understood the effects of the writer's methods; clearly understood links between text and ideas/context.

Answers

15–20 (Grade 3)	You have: given some explanation of the task; used references to support some comments; explained the writer's methods, sometimes using subject terminology; identified the effects of the writer's methods; understood some links between text and ideas/context.
8–14 (Grade 2)	You have: responded to the task and supported your response; commented on some references; identified the writer's methods; referred to subject terminology; shown awareness of some links between text and ideas/context.
1–7 (Grade U-1)	You have: responded to the task with simple comments; referred to some details; shown awareness that the writer has made choices; referred to subject terminology; made a simple comment on ideas/context.

Your answers could include some of the following points.

1. *Macbeth*
    As he reacts, his speech is broken up by caesuras; he asks a series of short questions, seeming not to believe the news; he accepts Malcolm's advice but asserts he must 'feel it like a man'; the scene gives Macduff the personal motivation to seek revenge; he gains sympathy as a family man and for showing his feelings; earlier he has passed Malcolm's 'test' by showing his own integrity; he is seen as loyal and brave, as Macbeth was at the start of the play; he fights bravely and fiercely and is patriotic and loyal to Malcolm; unlike Macbeth, he is honest and neither cruel nor ambitious; when he kills Macbeth we learn he was 'from his mother's womb/Untimely ripped', so the witches' prophecy can be true.

2. *Romeo and Juliet*
    Friar Laurence is surprised and shocked by Romeo saying he loves Juliet; he sees Romeo (and all young men) as fickle, their love 'not truly in their hearts, but in their eyes'; he recalls how love for Rosaline made Romeo miserable; his old love was read by 'rote', implying it was not real but like something from a story; he distinguishes between 'doting' and 'loving', not believing Romeo truly loved Rosaline; Juliet returns Romeo's love – 'Doth grace for grace and love for love allow'; Friar Laurence might not be convinced but sees an opportunity for reconciling the Capulets and Montagues; Romeo and Juliet's love is seen as strong and mutual when they meet; love is also complete when they marry, giving spiritual and sexual fulfilment; however, it puts them in opposition to their families, leading to their deaths.

3. *The Tempest*
    Caliban does not seem to want freedom, just a different master; he is servile, not defiant as he was before; all the characters are drunk and the scene is broadly comic; however, Caliban unexpectedly speaks in verse and describes the island poetically; perhaps this shows what he could have been if Prospero had not enslaved him – or perhaps his eloquence is the result of the education Prospero gave him; Caliban sings about his freedom. His joy might be genuine but he is not actually free; the play is influenced by the colonisation of places like America going on at the time, with settlers enslaving indigenous peoples; Caliban and Ariel are sometimes seen as two different kinds of slave; Prospero also enslaves Ferdinand to test his love; in a sense, all the characters are imprisoned on the island and most are freed at the end.

4. *Much Ado About Nothing*
    He is Don Pedro's brother but, as a bastard, is an outsider with no power; he claims that he is honest and will not pretend to gain favour; this is the first time we see him – he is talking to his confidant, Conrad, so we can take what he says as the truth; Conrad urges him to co-operate now he has been defeated by Don Pedro; they both use natural imagery – Conrad talks about a 'harvest' but Don John of being 'a canker in a hedge'; we will see later the use he makes of his discontent as he plots against Claudio and Hero; his actions provide the plot of the play, both by causing Claudio to reject Hero and, indirectly, bringing Beatrice and Benedick together; his presence casts a shadow over the play. He stands apart from the happiness of the others at the end; he can be seen as a 'malcontent', an unhappy character at odds with the world, common in plays of the time.

5. *The Merchant of Venice*
    Portia is in control here, telling Bassanio what she wants; however, she is controlled by the will of her dead father; she is obedient to her father's wishes, not wanting to be 'forsworn'; making a good marriage is important to her as well as to her father, but she wants to marry the man she loves; she speaks openly of her love for Bassanio while stating that 'a maiden hath no tongue but thought', meaning she has no real power; Jessica, like Portia, is controlled by her father but she asserts her independence by eloping; Portia and Nerissa disguise themselves as men. This is necessary if Portia is to be taken seriously; all three women express themselves openly and behave independently, following their hearts.

6. *Julius Caesar*
    Brutus's suicide would be seen as honourable by Romans; Antony makes a distinction between Brutus and the others – 'only he' had 'honest' motives; he is seen as a good politician, interested in 'common good to all'; he is also praised as a man – he was 'gentle' and he lacked the vice of envy; Antony uses rhetoric to proclaim Brutus's worth, imagining nature itself praising him; Octavius echoes Antony's sentiments,

wanting him treated 'according to his virtue'. Their sentiments are especially important because they were his enemies; in his conversations with Cassius, Brutus is shown as the idealist, an honourable man; he is important to the conspiracy because of his reputation; he is a brave soldier and leader who inspires love and loyalty.

7. *Henry V*

(a) Consciousness of reality of theatre (the 'wooden O') and the need for imagination; the speech paints a vivid picture of war and battles; use of rhetorical questions and other rhetorical devices, including assuming a (false?) modesty about what is to come; build-up of excitement and anticipation; speech assumes some knowledge of 'warlike Harry' and his achievements, which are to be celebrated.

(b) Henry seeks to carve himself a place in history by conquering France; he is seen as a unifying force, commanding respect and devotion; he invokes patriotism and becomes identified with England: 'God for Harry! England and Saint George!'; his victories make England influential and his marriage brings peace; at the end the Chorus reminds us, however, that his achievements were short lived.

8. *Othello*

(a) Iago, as elsewhere, takes the audience into his confidence; in doing this he is like the devils of medieval drama, involving us in his plans; the audience would feel sympathy for Othello, as even Iago admits his 'constant, loving nature'; he claims to be motivated by Othello's supposed adultery with Emilia. Does he really believe it? Would the audience believe it?; he teases the audience about what he will do next; here Iago raises the possibility that he is jealous (as well as envious) of Othello;

(b) Jealousy can be seen as Othello's 'fatal flaw', leading to his downfall; it is clear that his jealousy has no grounds and Desdemona is innocent; Othello's jealousy is so strong he loses trust in Desdemona and cannot see reason; jealousy is the result of the strength of his love for her; perhaps he also feels insecure in his marriage because of 'outsider' status, the result of his ethnicity.

9. *Twelfth Night*

(a) Orsino implies there can be no equal love between a man and a woman; he uses imagery of eating to compare a woman's love with his; the audience is aware that Viola loves him, creating dramatic irony in the scene; Viola, disguised as a man, tells of her love as if it were her sister's; her secret love seems more genuine and heartfelt than Orsino's 'hungry' love;

(b) Orsino's love for Olivia is seen as a self-indulgent 'pose' from the start; Olivia's 'love' for Cesario creates comic confusion as well as being clearly hopeless; Orsino and Olivia very quickly fall in love with the 'right' people so order can be restored; the trick played on Malvolio gives a broader comic version of unrequited love; mutual, returned love between a man and a woman is seen as the ideal, and is achieved in the end.

Pages 28–32: The Nineteenth Century Novel

Look at the mark scheme on page 72 for Shakespeare.
[Maximum 40 marks]
Your answers could include some of the following points.

1. *The Strange Case of Dr Jekyll and Mr Hyde*
In this chapter Jekyll is the narrator so we see the story from his point of view; he emphasises the potential dangers of the experiment; given the risks and the fact that he is experimenting on himself, the reader might admire Jekyll's actions; the description of the experiment is cool and factual but not detailed – no ingredients are named; the second paragraph focuses on Jekyll's reactions, carefully recorded but dramatic and disturbing; he brings together the worlds of science and morality, trying to separate good and evil; the experiment quickly becomes out of control as Hyde takes over; although Jekyll is using chemicals and transforming physically, the novel is more about psychology; Jekyll could be seen as 'playing God', interfering with nature in an unacceptable way, which is bound to end in tragedy.

2. *A Christmas Carol*
Scrooge is reluctant to go with the spirit but is less aggressive and uncooperative than before; the ghost is gentle but firm in making Scrooge go with him; Scrooge wants the ghost to put on his cap not knowing why – perhaps he is resisting the light of knowledge; the ghost reassures him that he has come to help him but Scrooge is nervous; the darkness vanishes and it is a 'clear, cold, winter day'. Scrooge will see things more clearly; Dickens uses these scenes to show how experience has changed Scrooge psychologically – his character the result of nurture, not nature; his lack of love as a child and the death of Fan explain his lack of feeling and his attitude to his nephew; he also made bad choices. He could have been like Mr Fezziwig as a boss and he could have married if he had not worshipped money; other characters, like the Cratchits, are shown not to be embittered by bad experiences; the ghosts show Scrooge that he can make choices and change for the better.

3. *Great Expectations*
The adult Pip is critical of his old ideas: 'I am afraid…'; he makes his younger self seem ridiculous for feeling even the stars were 'poor and humble'; Pip is aware of the difference the new clothes might make to how people look at him; Joe and Biddy have a different view, wanting to impress people with the new 'genteel' Pip; he dismisses the people of his own class as 'coarse and common', showing that he is becoming snobbish; Biddy shows awareness of his attitudes, almost tricking him into doing the right thing; his attitude confuses him but he is drawn to what he sees as a 'better' life; throughout the novel Pip gets into trouble because of his naïve belief in the

superiority of people from higher social classes; the reader can see the worth of characters like Joe and Biddy – representatives of the working class; Dickens exposes good and bad in all classes as Pip learns what is really of value in life.

4. *Jane Eyre*
The description of the 'gray old house of God' gives a sense of its importance and permanence, the building representing the idea of religion; Jane is aware of the significance of everything in the 'quiet and humble temple', this description reflecting her own nature; the words of the service about 'impediment' are given in full; the interruption is shocking and dramatic, breaking the atmosphere; Rochester is happy to go ahead in the knowledge that he is deceiving Jane and their marriage would not be 'lawful'; the fact that this happens in the church shows the extent of Rochester's deceit and the chasm between his and Jane's beliefs; Jane uses the language of religion throughout the novel and has a strong faith; although she is independently minded, her behaviour is always guided by her beliefs; she cannot agree to be Rochester's mistress because of her moral attitude; she can be critical of others who profess religious belief, however, especially if they are hypocrites; the religious fervour and goodness of St John Rivers are attractive to her but she realises that she cannot love him or dedicate herself to missionary work.

5. *Frankenstein*
Frankenstein consciously seeks spiritual comfort or inspiration in the mountains; the detailed description of his climb is in the present tense and reads almost like a travel guide; the place and the weather reflect his mood – pathetic fallacy – and he is aware of this; there is a sense of danger in the steep climb, increased by the bad weather, giving the reader a sense of there being something dramatic to come; the scene causes him to reflect on the nature of man; here and elsewhere the attitude to nature is in the Romantic tradition; descriptions of the vastness and magnificence of natural scenes give a sense of there being a power greater than man, whether God or nature itself; Frankenstein's experiment can be seen as interfering with nature in a way that must end in tragedy; the experiences of the creature focus on nature in a different sense – the nature v. nurture debate.

6. *Pride and Prejudice*
Extreme contrast in reactions of Mr and Mrs Bennet; Mrs Bennet saw Mr Collins as a good match for Elizabeth so she is disappointed; although expressed in a comic way, getting her daughters married is a serious issue; Mr Bennet's 'tranquil' response is more reasonable but reflects his refusal to take his wife's concerns seriously; seeing Charlotte as more foolish than his daughter is ironic as, in fact, Charlotte's decision is sensible and practical; both parents have favourites – Mr Bennet prefers Elizabeth to the others;

as a father he is loving (at least to Elizabeth) but rather distant and selfish; Mrs Bennet is overbearing and embarrassing but sees herself as working for her daughters' happiness; parent/child relationships must be seen in the context of the social and economic position of the girls and their dependence on their father and their future husbands.

7. *The Sign of Four*
The first person narrative gives immediacy and the readers see only what Watson sees; the relationship between the two men provides a light-hearted contrast to the mystery; Watson reports Holmes's speech, showing his brilliance and his arrogance; 'A Study in Scarlet' was Conan Doyle's last novel and Holmes's reaction to it would amuse readers; Watson shares his hurt and annoyance with the reader; Watson is anxious to be valued but Holmes seems unable to compliment or flatter him; Holmes's analysis of the small brochure is harsh but honest, contrasting with Watson's false modesty; Watson mentions his wound – his military and medical experience give him credibility as an observer; elsewhere Watson incorporates other characters' narratives; Watson can be seen as representing the average intelligent reader.

8. *The War of the Worlds*
The passage starts by addressing the reader – anxious to get the message across; uses extended metaphor of water to describe people fleeing; precise about times and places, as if writing a report; describes the violence caused by panic – 'revolvers were fired, people stabbed'; there is no organisation and/or control; here people are not given names or distinguished but elsewhere the experience of individuals is described; the narrator reports his own and others' experiences, especially his brother's account of events in London; he shows panic bringing out the worst in people but also some good as people try to help each other; his account of his own flight shows him to be more thoughtful than most, planning his actions carefully and not panicking.

9. *Silas Marner*
He has had no relationship with Eppie until now. She considers Silas her father; he says very little in response to Eppie's rejection. His feelings are implied; he is frustrated in his desire to put things right; Nancy speaks on his behalf, saying Eppie has a 'duty' to her 'lawful' father; Nancy supports and helps him in spite of his actions, showing a strong love between them; Nancy's reactions are informed by her mourning for her own child and her desire to be a mother; throughout the book he is shown as a good man and a good husband, who is haunted by his secret past; he is conscious of how he failed both Eppie and her mother; his first marriage is seen as a mistake and his second a success, but he cannot escape his past failings; at the end he accepts Eppie's decision and there is a feeling that he and Nancy learn to live with it.

Pages 33–36: Modern Texts

Look at the mark scheme on page 72 for Shakespeare.
[Maximum 40 marks]
Your answers could include some of the following points.

1. *An Inspector Calls*
    Priestley presents a very unequal society – we see the rich middle-class Birlings and hear about Eva Smith; Eva experiences many problems, such as losing her job and getting pregnant; at the time the play is set there is little help for her; Priestley wrote the play in the 1940s when there was a lot of discussion about the welfare state; Eva could be several different girls with different problems; she is a device for bringing them to our attention; her problems can be seen in terms of socialism and/or feminism. Are they the result of her class or her gender?; the central message is about taking responsibility for each other.

2. *Blood Brothers*
    Mrs Johnston makes a choice to give away (or sell) her child; her choice may be justified by her economic circumstances; there is a sense that tragedy is inevitable, expressed by the narrator; is this because of what she has done or because of class and poverty?; Mickey is seen as the victim of social inequality; however, he makes bad choices throughout the play; the writer's (and audience's) sympathies seem to be entirely with Mrs Johnston and Mickey; the two boys are not different in nature – their differences are the result of upbringing.

3. *The History Boys*
    The headmaster sees education as a competition – the boys' success reflects on the school; he is not an academic high-flyer and is in awe of Oxford and Cambridge; he does not give away what he really thinks about issues such as Hector's 'fiddling'; he has a distant relationship with the teachers and pupils. Teachers call him 'Headmaster'; he uses the teachers and manipulates them, especially Irwin against Hector; in turn he is manipulated and controlled by Dakin; his public language is formal and authoritative (as in his last speech) while in private it is coarse; he could be seen as being interested in self-preservation and taking credit for others' efforts.

4. *DNA*
    All the characters are teenagers. We are in their world; the 'killing' of Adam is shocking and shows what they are capable of; their reaction, blaming the postman, might be more shocking; they are part of a gang/friendship group but also belong to smaller groups; the interaction between them and the way they talk is typically 'teenage' – normal in spite of the abnormality of their actions; their relations with adults are not shown, only reported by them, but seem distant; they are distinct characters with different reactions, so not just stereotypical teenagers; they are dominated by strong characters and the demands of the group.

5. *The Curious Incident of the Dog in the Night-Time*
    'I find people confusing': Christopher articulates his perspective on the world; he speaks differently from other characters, saying what he thinks without embellishment; other characters are conscious of treating him differently, e.g. not touching him; his relationship with Siobhan marks him out as 'officially' different as in having special needs; his parents demonstrated how his 'difference' affects those close to him; his thoughts are presented through Siobhan reading his notes; the way he experiences life is presented theatrically, e.g. by the voices when he arrives at the station.

6. *A Taste of Honey*
    The play is centred on Jo and Helen, the men being incidental characters; Jo's relationships with men may be a reaction to her mother's attitudes; Helen uses men for money and sex. She depends on them but does not respect them; Jo's relationship with the boy is romantic but brief; he lets her down, shattering her dreams; the boy and Geof are outsiders (like Jo), one because of race and the other because of sexuality; Peter, the one man who is not an outsider, is unpleasant and overbearing; all the men leave Jo in the end, leaving her with Helen and facing an independent but uncertain future.

7. *Lord of the Flies*
    Simon is the opposite of Jack. He is inherently good; He is gentle, and kind to the little 'uns; he has the same sort of background as the other boys but for him ideas about morality and civilisation are not superficial; he understands what the 'beast' means; his hallucinations are almost mystical and holy; His murder represents the ultimate triumph of evil and savagery; he can be seen as a sacrificial victim, perhaps like Jesus.

8. *Telling Tales*
    At first the narrator seems to have a good relationship with his father as they go fishing together; they co-operate and work well together; fishing is part of a disappearing way of life, reflecting the change that will come for the family; when he overhears his father talking about Korea, the boy realises how his father feels towards him; the older generation seem to think more of themselves and money than of their children; compare with the distance between father and son in 'A Family Supper'; compare with the discovery of cruelty and violence in the older generation in 'The Darkness Out There'; compare the two narrators and their reactions in 'Korea' and 'Chemistry'.

9. *Animal Farm*
    Old Major is 'wise' and respected by the other animals so his ideas are listened to; he makes a logical and persuasive case against Man. He sounds reasonable; his 'dream' gives an almost mystical power to his ideas; although he talks about rebellion he does not make any practical plans for it and says it might not come for a long time; he is the equivalent of Karl Marx, whose ideas shaped communism; he dies before the rebellion so we

Answers

cannot know whether he would have remained an idealist; it is up to others to put his ideas into practice and interpret them; after the rebellion his ideas are changed and his followers corrupted; this reflects the history of the USSR and other regimes based on egalitarian ideals.

10. *Never Let Me Go*
She is a first person narrator and we see everything through her eyes; she is a naïve narrator as she does not understand a lot of what is happening; her tone is chatty, and she shares her feelings and reactions openly; she is proud of her success as a 'carer', working within the system; she herself is not quick to question but she listens to Tommy; her naïvety and lack of understanding mean that we discover things gradually with her; she forms strong emotional relationships, demonstrating her humanity.

11. *Anita and Me*
Syal describes Indian dress and food in great detail; the narrator is very aware of her 'different' culture; the visits of the aunts and uncles and Nanima bring Indian culture to Tollington; Meena is not always happy with being different and is drawn to the culture of Tollington; religion is part of the culture but is not as important to Meena's parents as to others; the stories told by her family give Meena a sense of culture, tradition and history; at the end, when they move, she embraces Indian culture and her ethnic identity more fully.

12. *Pigeon English*
The novel opens with a murder and Harrison becomes obsessed with 'the dead boy'; he witnesses the violent attack on Mr Frimpong and is drawn into a world of violent gangs; at first he is excited by violence, as if it wasn't real, but comes to understand the reality of it; there is violence in school and among teenagers outside school; Aunty Sonia has harmed herself to stay in the country; Miquita suffers violence from her boyfriend; it is a world of gangs, knives and guns – even the police on the tube are said to have guns; the climax, with Harrison himself being murdered, seems inevitable.

13. *Hobson's Choice*
Maggie's interest in Willie is a surprise to everyone except her; she says she sees him as a business proposition; the difference in class and his lack of education make it an unlikely match; at first it might appear that she just wants to marry anyone, so as not to be an 'old maid'; Willie is frightened of Maggie at first and does not love her; Maggie is the dominant partner in a reversal of social norms, creating comedy; their relationship is contrasted with those of Maggie's sisters, which are more conventionally romantic; after marriage Willie becomes an equal partner; he stands up to Hobson but it is only when he stands up to

Maggie that we feel their marriage is an equal one and they are in love.

14. *Journey's End*
The play exposes the reality of the First World War in a naturalistic way; it focuses on the effects of war on individuals but does not show any fighting; characters react to the stresses of war in different ways; there is no anti-war rhetoric in the play; however, it also lacks patriotic rhetoric or any justification for war; the play focuses on fear and those who are afraid are sympathetically drawn; there are positive aspects in the comradeship and commitment of the characters; at the time it was written many in the audience would not be aware of the reality of the trenches so the play might change their thinking.

15. *My Mother Said I Never Should*
(a) The speech conveys Doris's excitement and happiness at the prospect of marriage; she is also excited about getting on in her career; this speech is at the end of the play so the audience knows that she will sacrifice career for family; this is typical for women of her age and the play implicitly criticises that world;
(b) Margaret also has a conflict between work and marriage, focusing on work when her marriage fails; Jackie rejects marriage in favour of career. Could she be successful and happy if she had married?; women are seen as victims of society and men.

16. *The Woman in Black*
Eel House is isolated and cut off, giving a sense of loneliness and vulnerability; Hill uses imagery, e.g. 'like a ship at sea' to convey a sense of danger; descriptions of the weather add to this. The weather is actually dangerous; the weather is also used to reflect the narrator's feelings (pathetic fallacy); in this passage Kipps rationalises and momentarily banishes his fear; his memories of a different, happier place create a sense of calm, lowering tension before it is heightened; Eel House is a conventional setting for a ghost story in the Gothic tradition; however, the real tragedy occurs in a pleasant, apparently safe place.

17. *Oranges Are Not the Only Fruit*
Jeanette's mother is committed to an evangelical, Old Testament form of Christianity; their church is central to their lives and forms a community different from the rest of the town; Mrs Winterson is eccentric in her religious practice as in everything else; religion is written about with humour and Jeanette looks back affectionately on it; Bible stories and things like the missionary map appeal to the creative child; preaching and the Bible are of huge importance to Jeanette – but is it faith or a love of literature and 'showing off'?; Jeanette's sexuality is not accepted by the church and she cannot stay in the church; religion can be oppressive and cruel.

Pages 37–38: Poetry

For questions **1–6**, look at the mark scheme below **[Maximum 20]**.
For questions **7–9**, mark each part **(a)** and **(b)** out of **[20]**. For part **(b)**, ignore the first point about comparing texts/making comparisons.

Marks	Skills
17–20 (Grade 8–9)	You have: compared texts in an exploratory and critical way; used precise, appropriate references to support your interpretation; analysed the writers' methods using subject terminology appropriately; explored the effects of the writers' methods; explored links between text and ideas/context.
14–16 (Grade 6–7)	You have: made thoughtful, developed comparisons; used appropriate references to support your interpretation; examined the writers' methods using subject terminology effectively; examined the effects of the writers' methods; thoughtfully considered links between text and ideas/context.
11–13 (Grade 4–5)	You have: made clear comparisons; used references effectively to support your explanation; explained the writers' methods clearly using relevant subject terminology; understood the effects of the writers' methods; clearly considered the links between text and ideas/context.
8–10 (Grade 3)	You have: explained your comparisons; used references to support your comments; explained some of the writers' methods using some relevant subject terminology; explained the effects of the writers' methods; made some relevant links between text and ideas/context.
4–7 (Grade 2)	You have: responded to the texts and compared them; commented on references; identified some of the writers' methods using some subject terminology; identified some effects of the writers' methods; made some links between text and ideas/context.
1–3 (Grade U-1)	You have: commented on the texts; referred to some details; are aware of the writer making choices and may have used some subject terminology; attempted to comment on the effects of the writers' methods; attempted to make links between text and ideas/context.

Depending on which poem you chose to compare, your answer might include the following points.

1. • The poet associates memories with a place – 'Neutral Tones', 'Winter Swans', 'Letters from Yorkshire'.
   • Imagery of nature – 'When We Two Parted', 'Love's Philosophy', Sonnet 29, 'The Farmer's Bride', 'Winter Swans', 'Neutral Tones'.
   • Parent/child relationships – 'Follower', 'Walking Away', 'Mother, any distance', 'Before You Were Mine'.
   • Sense of another time expressed through detail – 'Before You were Mine', 'Follower', 'Walking Away'.
   • Sense of mortality – 'Neutral Tones', 'Follower'.
   • Use of natural imagery – 'Neutral Tones', 'Love's Philosophy', 'Winter Swans', 'The Farmer's Bride'.
   • Use of rhyme/half rhyme – 'Walking Away', 'Follower'.
   • Form and structure – regular quatrains with 'footnote' at the end.

2. • Account of a battle/war – 'The Charge of the Light Brigade', 'Exposure', 'Remains'.
   • Focus on suffering of individuals – 'Exposure', 'War Photographer', 'The Emigrée'.
   • The experience of the soldier – 'Exposure', 'Remains', 'Poppies', 'Kamikaze', 'The Charge of the Light Brigade'.
   • Ideas about patriotism and country – 'The Charge of the Light Brigade', 'Poppies', 'Kamikaze', 'Checking Out Me History', 'Exposure'.
   • Imagery from nature – 'Exposure', 'The Prelude', 'Storm on the Island', 'Kamikaze'.

• Death and mortality –'Remains', 'Exposure', 'War Photographer'.
• Use of past tense – 'The Charge of the Light Brigade', 'Remains', 'Kamikaze' – contrast 'Exposure'.
• Structure – three long stanzas, free verse – compare and contrast 'The Charge of the Light Brigade', 'Exposure', 'War Photographer', 'Remains'.

3. • Use of an extended metaphor – 'She Walks in Beauty', 'The Manhunt'.
   • Imagery from nature (here, water) – 'She Walks in Beauty', 'Neutral Tones', 'Nettles', 'La Belle Dame Sans Merci'.
   • Imagery used to explain feelings to loved one – Sonnet 43, '1st Date', 'Neutral Tones', 'I wanna be yours', 'Valentine'.
   • Contrast with imagery used for comic effect – 'I wanna be yours', 'Valentine'.
   • Helps create a sense of loss and sadness – 'Neutral Tones', 'One Flesh', 'La Belle Dame Sans Merci', 'The Manhunt'.
   • Imagery used to convey a change in feelings – 'Neutral Tones', 'One Flesh'.
   • Three six-line stanzas, with regular metre and rhyme scheme each developing the image – controlled emotion.

4. • An individual caught up in a violent situation – 'Exposure', 'The Man He Killed', 'War Photographer'.
   • Imagery used to describe feelings – here, language – 'Exposure', 'A Poison Tree', 'Half-Caste', 'Poppies'.

- Sense of powerlessness – 'Exposure', 'War Photographer'.
- Form used to convey excitement and danger – 'The Charge of the Light Brigade', 'The Destruction of Sennacherib'.
- Link to 'The Charge of the Light Brigade' and ideas of Empire through streets' names.
- A sense of ordinary life changed through violence and war – 'What Were They Like?', 'Poppies', 'Exposure'.
- First person experience of violence – 'War Photographer', 'The Man He Killed'.
- Ideas about identity and belonging – 'What Were They like?', 'Half-Caste', 'The Class Game', 'No Problem'.
- Use of enjambment – lack of control – contrast 'The Destruction of Sennacherib', 'The Charge of the Light Brigade'.

5.
- The poet visits or remembers a place with past associations – 'Where the Picnic Was', 'Adlestrop', 'Nothing's Changed', 'Home Thoughts from Abroad'.
- Place associated with feelings for another person 'Where the Picnic Was'.
- 'Descriptions of nature – 'To Autumn', 'Stewart Island', 'Adlestrop', 'Home Thoughts from Abroad', 'In Romney Marsh'.
- Contrast between peaceful place and violent feelings – 'Stewart Island', 'Nothing's Changed'.
- Compare and contrast poet's feelings with feelings in 'Composed upon Westminster Bridge', 'Where the Picnic Was', 'Adlestrop', 'Home Thoughts from Abroad'.
- Regular form and rhyme scheme, controlling emotion – 'London', 'Adlestrop'.
- Violent imagery ('earthquake') – 'In Romney Marsh', 'Stewart Island', 'London'.

6. (a)
- The poem is set at the end of summer; the changing seasons become a metaphor for getting older.
- The poet observes the lives of others.
- From watching the mothers and children at play he imagines their home lives.
- The life described is a typical/stereotypical married life of the time (1959).
- There is a tone of nostalgia and sadness about passing time.

(b)
- Compare 'Death of a Naturalist', about growing up, with contrasting violent imagery.
- Compare 'Ozymandias', about time and mortality, but on a grand, not domestic, scale.
- Compare 'Cozy Apologia', where the poet reminisces about younger days but expresses content with the present.

7. (a)
- 'Repetition of 'I remember, I remember' at the start of each stanza.
- Short lines and rhyme give a childish feel to the poem.

- Words like 'little' and 'peeping' add to the sentimental view of childhood.
- Memories all involve literal imagery in descriptions of nature.
- He looks back on his childhood as a time of pure happiness.
- Each stanza, except for the third, contrasts his happy memory with his feelings now.
- Childhood seen from the point of view as an older, sick person.
- There is a lot of colour (in the second stanza) and movement (in the third), giving a sense of a child's wonder and enthusiasm for life.
- The regularity of metre and rhyme scheme contain his emotions, both joyful and sad.
- The last four lines almost dismiss childhood experience ('It was a childish ignorance') and reflect on how he has changed.
- He does not explain why he thinks he is 'farther off from Heaven'. What sort of life has he led?
- 'Past and Present' is about the distant past of childhood while 'Love After Love' is about recent adult experiences.
- Walcott uses the second person, as if he is giving advice to someone. Hood uses the first person.
- Walcott focuses on the future.
- He feels things will get better, while Hood does not see a future for himself.
- Walcott uses semi-religious images of feasting and celebration.
- Irregular structure; use of enjambment and caesura; broken up, thoughtful and natural speech.

(b)
- Other poems you might write about, focusing on how poets write about the past, include 'A Song', 'A Broken Appointment', 'An Arundel Tomb', 'Long Distance II' and 'Now'.

8. (a)
- 'Repetition of 'I remember, I remember' at the start of each stanza.
- Short lines and rhyme give a childish feel to the poem.
- Memories all involve literal imagery in descriptions of nature.
- He looks back on his childhood as a time of pure happiness, implying that he is now old and not as happy.
- Each stanza, except for the third, contrasts his happy memory with his feelings now.
- Childhood seen from the point of view as an older, sick person.
- There is a lot of colour (in the second stanza) and movement (in the third), giving a sense of a child's wonder and enthusiasm for life.
- The regularity of metre and rhyme scheme contain his emotions, both joyful and sad.
- The last four lines almost dismiss childhood experience ('It was a childish ignorance') and reflect on how he has changed.

- He does not explain why he thinks he is 'farther off from Heaven'. What sort of life has he led? Is he now thinking about his death?
- Dickinson does not seem to be ill or as old as Hood.
- The poem appears to be about the winter but the winter light is an image of death.
- An everyday experience ('a certain slant of light') makes her think of death.
- It is ever-present in the everyday.
- The sense of death 'oppresses' her; Hood is more aware of his feelings about life.
- She uses a series of unusual images to try to define the feeling.
- The shortness of the lines and use of dashes give the impression of breathlessness.
- A simple form; four stanzas of equal length and a regular rhyme scheme.

(b)
- Other poems you might write about, focusing on how the poets write about death and mortality, include 'The Man He Killed', 'Anthem for Doomed Youth', 'Punishment', 'Honour Killing' and 'Lament'.

9. (a)
- 'Repetition of 'I remember, I remember' at the start of each stanza.
- Short lines and rhyme give a childish feel to the poem.
- Words like 'little' and 'peeping' add to the sentimental view of childhood.
- Memories all involve literal imagery in descriptions of nature.
- He looks back on his childhood as a time of pure happiness.

- Each stanza, except for the third, contrasts his happy memory with his feelings now.
- Childhood seen from the point of view as an older, sick person.
- There is a lot of colour (in the second stanza) and movement (in the third), giving a sense of a child's wonder and enthusiasm for life.
- The regularity of metre and rhyme scheme contain his emotions, both joyful and sad.
- The last four lines almost dismiss childhood experience ('It was a childish ignorance') and reflect on how he has changed.
- He does not explain why he thinks he is 'farther off from Heaven'. What sort of life has he led?
- Clarke's memories are darker and more disturbing.
- However, she too seems to be happy as a child in her own relationships.
- The poem tells the story of an incident involving a 'dead child'.
- There are elements of fairy tale and biblical imagery.
- She uses natural imagery.
- Memories are important, as with Hood, but she feels memories are unreliable.
- There is an awareness of mortality.
- The stanzas are of unequal length with no rhyme.
- The memory disturbs her and makes her reflect on time and memory.

(b)
- Other poems you might write about, focusing on how poets write about childhood, include, 'Red Roses', 'Midnight on the Great Western' 'Spring and Fall: to a Young Child' and 'Baby Song'.

Pages 39–40: Unseen Poetry

1. [Maximum of [20].

Marks	Skills
17–20 (Grade 8–9)	**(a)** You have: explored the texts critically; used precise references to support your interpretation; analysed the writer's methods using appropriate subject terminology. **(b)** You have: critically compared the writers' use of language, structure and form, using appropriate subject terminology; convincingly compared the effects of the writers' methods on the reader.
14–16 (Grade 6–7)	**(a)** You have: responded thoughtfully to the text; used appropriate references to support your interpretation; examined the writer's methods using subject terminology effectively. **(b)** You have: thoughtfully compared the writers' use of language and/or structure and/or form, using effective subject terminology; thoughtfully compared the effects of the writers' methods on the reader.
11–13 (Grade 4–5)	**(a)** You have: responded clearly to the text; used references effectively to support your explanation; explained the writer's methods using relevant subject terminology; understood the effects of the writer's methods on the reader. **(b)** You have: clearly compared the writers' use of language and/or structure and/or form, using effective subject terminology; clearly compared the effects of the writers' methods on the reader.
8–10 (Grade 3)	**(a)** You have: explained your response to the text; used references to support your comments; explained some of the writer's methods using some relevant subject terminology; identified the effects of the writer's methods on the reader. **(b)** You have: made some relevant comparisons of the writers' use of language and/or structure and/or form, using effective subject terminology; made some comparisons of the effects of the writers' methods on the reader.

Answers

4–7 (Grade 2)	**(a)** You have: responded to the text; commented on references; identified some of the writer's methods using some subject terminology; commented on the effects of the writer's methods on the reader. **(b)** You have: made some links between the writers' use of language and/or structure and/or form, using effective subject terminology; made some links between the effects of the writers' methods on the reader.
1–3 (Grade U-1)	**(a)** You have: commented on the text; referred to some details; are aware of the writer making choices and may have used some subject terminology; attempted to comment on the effects of the writer's methods on the reader. **(b)** You may have: attempted to make links between the writers' use of language and/or structure and/or form, using subject terminology; attempted to make links between the effects of the writers' methods on the reader.

Your answer might include comments on:

(a) 'Repetition of 'I remember, I remember' at the start of each stanza; short lines and rhyme give a childish feel to the poem; words like 'little' and 'peeping' add to the sentimental view of childhood; memories all involve literal imagery in descriptions of nature; he looks back on his childhood as a time of pure happiness; each stanza, except for the third, contrasts his happy memory with his feelings now; childhood seen from the point of view as an older, sick person; there is a lot of colour (in the second stanza) and movement (in the third), giving a sense of a child's wonder and enthusiasm for life; the regularity of metre and rhyme scheme contain his emotions, both joyful and sad; the last four lines almost dismiss childhood experience ('It was a childish ignorance') and reflect on how he has changed; he does not explain why he thinks he is 'farther off from Heaven'. What sort of life has he led?

(b) The first is written by an older man looking back on childhood, the second from the child's point of view; when describing childhood experience, both express joy and excitement (both describing a swing); both describe nature (literal imagery): flowers, trees, cattle, etc; both seem to have safe, secure childhoods, contained in gardens; Stevenson's poem has no awareness of growing old; Stevenson's poem has a simple rhyme scheme and metre, like Hood's, but has shorter stanzas; Stevenson's sentiments are as simple as the form, unlike Hood's. It might be written for children.

English Literature Set B

Pages 42–46: Shakespeare

For all questions, look at the mark scheme for Set A, Shakespeare, on page 72. **[Maximum 40]**

Your answers could include the following points.

1. *Macbeth*
   (a) Repetition of 'blood' shows obsession with violence; 'Our great bidding' shows his pride as king – he expects obedience; he controls the country through spies; he is 'steeped in so far' that he will not turn back; he will become more ruthless; there is a sense that he is out of control, lacking sleep and having 'strange things' in his head.
   (b) The witches' prophecy makes him think about being king; at first he is unsure and has a conscience but Lady Macbeth pushes him into murdering Duncan; the murder of Banquo and attempt to murder Fleance show his increasing paranoia and ruthlessness; strange omens are reported and Scotland suffers under his reign; the murder of Lady Macduff and her children shows a new level of cruelty.

2. *Romeo and Juliet*
   (a) Here Juliet drinks the Friar's potion to avoid marrying Paris and to be united with Romeo; the fear she shows underlines how desperate and determined she is while reminding us of her youth; her imagination runs wild, as she contemplates the horror of waking in a tomb; her soliloquy is full of questions and caesuras, as one thought leads to another; the language is macabre and ghoulish, striking fear in the audience.
   (b) We know from the prologue that Juliet will die; Romeo and Juliet's love is doomed because of the violent feud between their families; Romeo's love for Juliet leads indirectly to the deaths of Tybalt and Mercutio; during the 'balcony' scene there are premonitions of death just as they are falling in love; the intensity of their love causes them to kill themselves; they are united in death.

3. *The Tempest*
   (a) Ferdinand plays on Miranda's name to express his admiration; he compares her to other women, judging her to be better than any he has seen; she admits that she is 'skilless' in judging men but cannot imagine anyone better; they see each other as ideals. He talks of virtues while she focuses on appearance; Ferdinand uses the word 'bondage' of love. He has just been enslaved by Prospero.
   (b) The main love relationship is between father and child, Prospero and Miranda; Miranda's only other experience of a man is Caliban, who assaulted her; elsewhere, relationships that should be based on love, between brothers, have broken down and must be mended; marriage is seen as important for reasons of politics as well as love; Miranda's innocence and purity (her 'dower') are emphasised; it is important that Ferdinand's intentions are honourable.

4. *Much Ado about Nothing*

The audience is aware of Hero and Ursula's plot to make Beatrice acknowledge her feelings; Beatrice's attempts to remain hidden (when in fact the others know she is there) provide comedy; Hero and Ursula's praise for Benedick is hyperbolic and intended for Beatrice's ears; Beatrice's closing soliloquy alerts us to her true feelings and intentions; here, trickery is used to reveal truth; in the masque, disguise allows people freedom to tell the truth; however it can also be used maliciously to deceive; Don John's trick, designed to make Claudio believe that Hero is unfaithful, works and almost causes tragedy; Claudio is tricked into thinking Hero is dead to make him realise that he loves her; the final trick has elements of magic and religious symbolism with Hero apparently brought back to life.

5. *The Merchant of Venice*

Here Shylock is seen imprisoning his daughter so sympathy would probably be for her; the language he uses when describing the masques makes him appear a killjoy; his anti-Christian sentiments ('Christian fools', etc.) might offend audiences; his stated intention to sack Lancelot makes him unsympathetic; however, Jessica's couplet at the end of the scene indicates that his fears for her are justified; consider the likely differences between Elizabethan and modern audience sympathies; audience sympathies are likely to be with Jessica when she elopes but might shift when Shylock hears about what she has done; when he insists on the 'pound of flesh' in court, audiences might be repelled; however, their sympathies might shift when he is humiliated at the end.

6. *Julius Caesar*

Brutus and Cassius are equal partners and both leaders. Here, cracks begin to show in their relationship; Cassius appears sensitive about his position – the 'wrong' is that he feels 'slighted'; Brutus is concerned more with ethics: Cassius should not have interfered with justice on behalf of a friend; Brutus accuses Cassius of having an 'itching palm', making the argument more personal; this brings a violent reaction from Cassius; Brutus takes the moral high ground, asserting that they killed Caesar for the sake of justice; Brutus's 'noble' reputation is important to Cassius as it attracts support for the conspiracy; their personalities are very different. Cassius is more pragmatic and wily; in spite of this they admire each other and have a warm friendship, shown when they make up after this argument, using affectionate language.

7. *Henry V*

(a) Just before this, Henry has expressed his anger and desire to be ruthless; Henry seems to expect defeat, asking if the herald has come for ransom; Mountjoy's speech paints a grim picture of the scene after a battle; the speech stresses how many men of all ranks have been killed; he refers several times to the amount of blood involved, conveying the horror of the scene; the image of the horses 'killing them twice' is very powerful; this speech might invoke sympathy for the French as victims, reminding the audience that war causes death and suffering on all sides; Henry is triumphant and praises God – throughout the play he claims God's support; the name 'Agincourt' would resonate for many in the audience, showing that this is the beginning of Henry's victory.

(b) Elsewhere Shakespeare shows the less glorious aspects of war – for example, looting and profiteering; the range of characters involved shows how war involves and affects all classes and all kinds of people.

8. *Othello*

(a) The audience is aware that Iago has told Othello that Desdemona is unfaithful; Desdemona is unaware of what he might be reading into her innocent words – dramatic irony; the audience would feel sympathy for Desdemona but perhaps also for Othello, knowing how Iago is manipulating him; Desdemona is confused by Othello's attitude – 'this is not a boon'; Othello's angry reaction after she leaves – 'Excellent wretch' – shows his emotional nature and his willingness to believe the worst; they both express their love in different ways – she says she is 'obedient'; he says there would be 'Chaos' without her.

(b) Their marriage has defied convention and, while there is love, there is a lack of understanding and trust; Iago and Emilia's marriage is also lacking in trust and honesty, though in their case there is little love; both husbands are quick to accuse their wives of unfaithfulness; Desdemona is faithful, obedient and loving, as a wife would be expected to be; Emilia is cynical about marriage: 'It is their husbands' faults/If wives do fall'.

9. *Twelfth Night*

(a) Orsino uses extravagant imagery and language to describe love; he uses an extended metaphor comparing music to food and a simile to compare the 'spirit of love' to the sea; he seems very concerned about the nature of love rather than the woman he supposedly loves; when he mentions Olivia he again uses word play ('the hart') to introduce another image; he focuses on the suffering caused by unrequited love, as Olivia herself focuses on her grief.

(b) Viola's arrival creates confusion and misunderstood emotions; she cannot express her love openly but talks of her 'sister' who pined away; when the characters finally fall in love with the 'right people' there is far less talk about emotions; as well as romantic/sexual love we see love for siblings: Viola and Sebastian are so close they are almost one; Toby's relationship with Maria provides a bawdy, comic version of love; unreturned love is seen as wasteful and pointless (as well as ridiculously comic and pathetic in Malvolio's case).

Pages 47–50: The Nineteenth Century Novel

Look at the mark scheme for Set A, Shakespeare on page 72. **[Maximum 40]**

Your answers could include some of the following points.

1. *The Strange Case of Dr Jekyll and Mr Hyde*
The description of the scene at twilight creates a sad, gentle mood; Jekyll is compared to a 'disconsolate prisoner', making him seem like a victim; Jekyll's words about being 'low' and it 'will not last long' suggest an illness he is not in control of; Jekyll is polite and pleasant when speaking to the visitors; the sudden change in his look is frightening and the 'horror and despair' is like the reaction of a victim; Jekyll is discussed by Utterson and Lanyon as someone who used to be a good, reasonable man but has become strange; his friends are inclined to see him as a victim of Hyde and want to help him; Dr Lanyon's narrative reveals the full horror of what Jekyll has become and his 'moral turpitude'; Jekyll's own narrative gives us insight into his motives and his feelings about what he has done, making him sympathetic again.

2. *A Christmas Carol*
The Cratchits show their love for Tim and for each other after the 'death' of Tiny Tim; Mrs Cratchit is anxious about Bob, not thinking of herself; Bob tries to be positive, speaking of the 'green place' where Tim is to be buried, but breaks down; contrast between reactions to Scrooge's death and Tiny Tim's; the reaction of Scrooge's nephew contrasts with how Scrooge treats people including the Cratchits; the Cratchits represent decent hard-working people who find it hard to get by; they are the model of a loving, cheerful family, and show the true spirit of Christmas; Scrooge's treatment of Bob shows him to be a bad employer, in contrast with his old boss Fezziwig; Scrooge learns from watching the Cratchits at home. Their home life is the opposite of his; sending the turkey to the Cratchits shows how much Scrooge has changed.

3. *Great Expectations*
(a) The setting in the graveyard makes Magwitch's first appearance terrifying and memorable; he is described as an intimidating figure and is clearly an escaped convict but his cold and hunger might make him sympathetic; his speech, rough both in content and style, is in stark contrast to Pip's; although frightening to young Pip, there is a comic element to the character brought out by the adult narrator; his physical strength is emphasised.
(b) He is absent for most of the novel and not even mentioned so that his reappearance comes as a surprise; Pip's reaction to discovering he is his benefactor puts Pip in an unsympathetic light – he mentions his 'abhorrence'; in contrast to Pip and his 'expectations', Magwitch has done well through his own hard work; Magwitch tells his own story, making him sympathetic and correcting a lot of Pip's misunderstandings; the fact that he could turn Pip into a gentleman – and that he is Estella's father – questions the idea of social class and privilege; he is like a father to Pip and Pip comes to see that he is a 'better man'.

4. *Jane Eyre*
Jane is included in the party but sits apart, listening, and not making a contribution; she slips out by a side-door, wanting to be as unobtrusive as possible; Rochester seems concerned about her but questions her abruptly; he also gives her orders, 'Return to the drawing-room'; she is conscious of not having the 'freedom' to speak to him as an equal; she is from an upper or upper-middle class background but is impoverished and has to earn a living; her position means that she can mix with (and observe) servants as well as employers and their friends; she does not like the affectations of people like the snobbish Ingrams; her judgments are not based on class – she can praise or condemn people regardless of their background; Rochester does not care about her class or background; ultimately, though, she returns to her 'proper' position in life, getting an inheritance as well as a 'good' marriage.

5. *Frankenstein*
(a) Frankenstein compares his enthusiasm to a 'hurricane' and there is a sense of violent haste about the account; he admits that pride and ambition motivate him; there is a sense of the virtue of pursuing knowledge, bringing 'a torrent of light into our dark world'; however, his language betrays a desire to 'play God' by becoming a 'creator'; his description of the 'horrors' of his work, digging up bones, etc., conveys a sense of revulsion at odds with his ideas about doing something noble; this is seen as 'profane' against religion and God, in desecrating holy ground.
(b) After giving the creature life, Frankenstein is instantly repelled and rejects his creation; he makes no attempt to care for or educate the creature, which therefore has to learn from its experience; he becomes afraid of the creature and remorseful about his actions; he is punished for his act of creation by the deeds of the creature and his own misery.

6. *Pride and Prejudice*
Austen describes Mr Collins's reaction ironically by using the kind of hyperbolic vocabulary he might have used – 'triumph', 'grandeur'; his 'triumph' depends on others ('his wondering visitors') being as snobbish; Sir William responds in the same way, showing off about his own 'situation in life', to assert his superiority to Mr Collins; Mr Collins assumes others will be as impressed as he is and keen that the experience does not 'overpower' them, the implication being that he hopes it does; his advice to Elizabeth about her dress is comic because of its inappropriateness – as a man he would not be expected to discuss such things with ladies; snobbery is shown by his concern

with superficial things like how people dress and how many rooms they have; what he says about Lady Catherine and the 'distinction of rank' proves to be true, showing that she is a snob; Darcy is also a snob, though not as obviously as his aunt. This is shown in his behaviour at the Meryton ball; Jane's romance with Bingley is almost ruined by the snobbery of Darcy and Bingley's sisters; perhaps Elizabeth might also be a bit of a snob. Consider her feelings about her family's behaviour at Netherfield Park.

7. *The Sign of Four*
Watson is excited about showing the treasure to Miss Morston and proud of being allowed to bring it; he may see the treasure as proof of his love for her; she has 'no eagerness in her voice', surprising us by her apparent 'indifference' to the treasure; tension and expectation are built by the description of the box and the difficulty of opening it; the treasure box is exotic and incongruous in Mrs Forrester's house, the use of Mrs Forrester's poker adding some humour; as soon as he sees the box is empty Watson feels relieved. The treasure was a 'golden barrier' between him and Miss Morston; the fact that she feels the same proves their mutual love; finding the treasure seemed to be the point of the adventure but solving the mystery and finding out the truth are more important; the pursuit of it has placed Holmes, Watson and others in 'horrible peril'; it is the motive for the killing of Jonathan Sholto and the reason for the death of Morston; the story of Jonathan Small shows that the Agra treasure – or rather the desire of people to possess it – has always caused unhappiness and death.

8. *The War of the Worlds*
(a) Wells uses the artilleryman to describe scenes the narrator does not experience; his account gives a different viewpoint – the view of someone who was involved in the battle; the story shows the powerlessness of humans against the Martians – the army can do nothing; as an individual he can only run away and hide; his disjointed account gives a series of images of frightened, fleeing people; the Martians' technology is described with a sense of wonder – it is far more advanced than anything on Earth; it is not a conventional war in any sense.
(b) Attempts to resist the Martians are feeble and futile; Wells describes the mental and physical effects on individuals, e.g. the artilleryman, the curate, as well as on groups; there are vivid descriptions of the destruction of buildings, towns and cities which might be familiar to the reader as peaceful, pleasant places (Weybridge, Richmond Hill); the accounts of the mass movement of fleeing people are reminiscent of many recent wars; there is uncertainty and confusion, even anarchy, after the invasion.

9. *Silas Marner*
(a) Eliot says that the 'misfortune' has shown Silas in a 'new light', implying that the villagers might enjoy seeing him brought down; they can now feel sorry for him, seeing his oddities as harmless 'craziness'; there

is real kindness as people bring him gifts, showing a sense of community; their kindness is associated with Christmas and, therefore, Christianity. Mr Crakenthorp draws a lesson from the robbery; some are just interested in hearing about the crime, wanting him to repeat the story; now that he has money he is more like one of them, 'no worse off nor other poor folks'; Eliot uses dialect to give a flavour of the villagers' speech.
(b) The attitudes of the Raveloe villagers are contrasted with those of people in Lantern Yard; Raveloe people might be said to act like Christians while the Lantern yard people claim to be religious but do not act in a Christian way; in her descriptions of The Rainbow, Eliot gives a sense of an English farming community of the early 19th century; it is a peaceful, fairly prosperous village, perhaps described nostalgically.

Pages 51–55: Modern Texts

Look at the mark scheme for Set A Shakespeare on page 72. **[Maximum 40]**

Your answers could include some of the following points.

1. *An Inspector Calls*
The Inspector takes charge and commands respect; he is an 'outsider' and does not belong to the world the Birlings move in; he acts like a detective in that he is investigating something and asking a lot of questions; he is not really investigating a crime but is looking into the reasons for Eva's act; he apportions blame and judges the other characters; he moralises about society and warns of the consequences of acting like the Birlings; his name, Goole, is pronounced the same as 'ghoul'. Is he a ghost from the future?; he has come from the 1940s, the time the play was written, to examine an earlier time; he may be warning the audience not to return to the society of 1912; he can be seen as the voice of the writer.

2. *Blood Brothers*
Linda stands up for Mickey to his brother and the other older children; she is one of the gang, equal to the boys in their games; she is protective and caring towards Mickey; the conversation about dying prefigures the end of the play, as does Sammy's gun; she is pragmatic in a comic childish way: 'if y'dead, there's no school'; here Mickey introduces Linda to Edward for the first time: their relationship will be crucial; in the park Linda proves better than the boys at shooting: is Russell making a feminist point?; she is outgoing and witty, and she helps to create a lighter atmosphere as she and the boys have fun together; she is in love with Mickey but, as his wife, is frustrated in her attempts to help him; she turns to Edward for help, unwittingly bringing the tragedy closer.

3. *The History Boys*
Mrs Lintott says Posner wants to know if Irwin has 'ceased to be a teacher and become a friend', implying

Answers

you cannot be both; Posner is looking for personal advice, which could be seen as part of a teacher's job; Irwin seeks to discover more about Hector's relationship with the boys; this could be seen as crossing a professional line or as showing concern about Hector crossing lines; Posner notices Irwin's interest in Dakin. Dakin takes advantage of this attraction and treats Irwin as if he were a friend; Hector blurs the lines between teacher/pupil relationships and friendship. Even without the 'groping' he could be seen as over-friendly; it could be said that a 'friendly' relationship with pupils is helpful in teaching but that is not the same as becoming friends; at times the friendship between staff and pupils can seem fun and positive but it can also be harmful and manipulative (on both sides).

4. *DNA*
They do not seem to have made any moral choice about the 'killing'. Things just got out of control; however, the act shows an inability to apply a sense of right and wrong; led by Phil, they make the choice to blame someone else for their actions; Leah talks about the bonobos and having empathy: empathy might be the closest they get to morality, but they do not usually apply it; they are concerned with self-preservation and will do anything to avoid getting into trouble; Lou and Danny have doubts about framing the postman but their concerns are mostly about the effect on them of being found out; towards the end, several characters suffer under the weight of guilt, e.g. Brian 'on medication', John Tate disappearing; at the end Leah tries to stand up for the truth but is not listened to and ends up leaving; the ending is bleak, with no sense of justice being done; at best their morality is relative. Some might say that, as a group, they were amoral.

5. *The Curious Incident of the Dog in the Night-Time*
Christopher is concerned by the fact that he has been accused of killing Wellington; he like facts and is not willing to let this go – he needs to know the truth; he applies his own logic to the case, based on dogs being as important as people; Ed's reaction suggests to the audience (but not to literal-minded Christopher) that he is hiding something; his investigation will lead him to uncover the truth about other things, like his parents' marriage; he becomes more independent, taking the initiative and facing his fears, e.g. on the train; other characters may begin to value him more. Does he value them more?; he himself attributes his increased confidence and success to the incident: 'I can because I went to London on my own.'; we are left wondering how much he can achieve ('Does that mean I can do anything?'); how much has he changed? And if he has not changed, does it matter?

6. *A Taste of Honey*
In the extract Jo seems unconcerned about how she will manage, as Geof questions her about money; she shows her immaturity and lack of understanding of what motherhood will mean; her attitude might be a way of avoiding her true feelings; she does not say she

wants to be a mother but refuses to consider abortion; she says she does not know much about love – will she be able to love the baby?; Geof, not knowing her, assumes Helen will care because she is Jo's mother; later she panics and says 'I don't want to be a mother'; Geof tries to help her but she reacts by joking and flirting, trying to avoid the subject of motherhood; Helen's idea of being a mother is unconventional. She is selfish and shows little concern for Jo; she becomes sentimental about the baby but focuses on material things like the cot; their love–hate relationship is the central one in both their lives.

7. *Lord of the Flies*
Being British or English is a shorthand for being civilised; the boys' ideas of correct behaviour are entwined with ideas about being British, learned at home and at public school; the officer talks about British boys putting on a 'better show'. Being British means coping with adversity; at the time the novel was written, Britain's place in the world was changing, the days of Empire coming to an end; the sense of 'Britishness' alluded to by the officer is a male upper class concept; the novel is influenced by the kind of boys' adventure stories popular in the 19th and early 20th centuries, in which British boys overcame danger and adversity; Britain is associated with colonialism – the events of the novel undermine the idea of colonialism; Golding implicitly criticises all nation states, not just Britain, and their involvement in wars.

8. *Telling Tales*
At the beginning, stories about crashed planes and girls being attacked are just rumours to Sandra, not reality; her walk to the cottage in the woods is reminiscent of a fairy tale; Mrs Rutter's story reveals the reality of war and death; the young people are shocked at how Mrs Rutter and her sister behaved; she sees Kerry differently because of his angry reaction: 'older and larger'; she feels that her life is changed and sees the 'darkness out there'; compare with the way in which the narrator learns about death and growing up in 'Chemistry'; compare with the change in the narrator's feelings about his father in 'Korea'; compare the change to Elizabeth's life in 'The Odour of Chrysanthemums'.

9. *Animal Farm*
Old Major blames humans for all the animals' problems; he states that 'we must not come to resemble them' and lists things that animals must never do; even when they are putting up the commandments, the pigs give instructions to the other animals; the pigs learn human skills and take privileges for themselves but Squealer stops opposition by threatening the return of humans; they breed dogs to keep order and they follow Napoleon as they did Mr Jones; the pigs start dealing with humans, using money and sleeping at the farmhouse, but have an answer for every criticism; the other animals change from being willing comrades and supporters to being confused and questioning, but they continue to obey the

Answers

pigs; the pigs eventually rule by terror and are more cruel than humans; at the end the pigs are indistinguishable from men, their transformation complete; these changes reflect the changes in the behaviour of leaders in communist and other populist regimes.

10. *Never Let Me Go*
Here, Ruth voices her feelings about being a clone, which no-one else has articulated; the word 'clone' is rarely used in the novel and for a long time the reader might not realise the characters are clones; Ruth feels that the others are living a fantasy, trying to make themselves feel better; she associates clones with 'trash' – they are even less than the worst humans; Kathy has hinted at their origins before and they may be right; in spite of the clones knowing that they are different, they have human emotions and human relationships; Kathy feels that their 'human' behaviour is learned, with her friends imitating relationships and behaviour they see on television; at the end her feelings are no different from the feeling of any human; we see everything through a clone's eyes, leading us to wonder what the difference is between clones and humans; we might ask whether it will be possible to create clones in this way and, if so, will they feel and think like humans?

11. *Anita and Me*
The house is described as old-fashioned and uncomfortable; Meena's father gets 'sick of it' and its distance from work; Tollington's situation in the countryside appeals to Meena's mother; she likes it because it reminds her of home in the Punjab; she is seen as unusual and odd by other Indians who want modern houses nearer the city; Tollington itself is a poor run-down village; part of its appeal to the young Meena is its size and the sense of community; the family is conscious of being the only Indian family and therefore the object of curiosity and prejudice; they are also middle class and better educated than most of their neighbours and they sometimes look down on them; as Meena gets older, she becomes more aware of racism and the differences between her and other Tollington people.

12. *Pigeon English*
Mamma is a dominant character in Harrison's life; she is seen as hard-working and caring, perhaps a stereotypical African mother; Aunty Sonia is a more disturbing figure. She is entertaining and fascinating but her self-harm is disturbing; Lydia is a stereotypical older sister, fighting with Harrison and bossing him around; his crush on Poppy gives some relief from the violence; women, such as Miquita and Aunty Sonia, are seen as victims of violence; although they are portrayed as strong personalities, they are largely ineffective; the gangs depicted are all male and the violence is mostly done by males; adult males, if not violent or criminal, do not feature much in Harrison's life.

13. *Hobson's Choice*
Willie is introduced as an unambitious worker with no education and no hope for advancement; Maggie sees his potential and is ambitious on his behalf; she is also ambitious for herself and sees their marriage as a business opportunity; Hobson has built himself a business but has no aspirations for it or for his children; Vicky and Alice aspire to better lives by marrying men who would be considered 'above' them socially; just as Willie cannot achieve without Maggie, both of them need Mrs Hepworth's help to succeed; however, their success is seen as mainly the result of hard work and dedication; Maggie can be seen as a 'new woman', independent and ambitious; their real achievement might be learning to love each other and be equal partners.

14. *Journey's End*
He is typical of officers in WWI, young and inexperienced with a public school background; his background is apparent in the way he speaks and what he talks about; he is respected by the men and other officers; the stress of war and responsibility lead to alcohol dependence; Raleigh hero-worships him but he finds his attitude hard to deal with; the older Osborne is protective, almost a father-figure; he reveals his fears, showing that they are natural and shared by all; he shows compassion for others; the audience would be aware that many men like him were killed.

15. *My Mother Said I Never Should*
(a) Margaret is in charge, picking up Rosie and taking her away; she does not give Jackie an opportunity to change her mind; Jackie talks to Rosie when she has already gone, expressing her feelings through the memories the clothes bring; she becomes 'hysterical' and shouts for her to come back; when she says 'Mummy' it is not clear who she is talking about.
(b) Margaret calls herself 'Mummy' to Rosie. But she confuses Rosie and Jackie; Jackie and Margaret continue to have a difficult relationship, Jackie's visits with expensive gifts causing tension; Margaret rebels against Doris, asserting her independence and telling her things are changing; Doris has an easier relationship with Rosie than any of the women have with their daughters.

16. *The Woman in Black*
The opening creates expectations as the telling of ghost stories leads Kipps to think about the 'real thing'; young Kipps's scepticism and rationality make the appearances seem more real; early appearances of the woman are brief and unexplained; the lonely situation and the appearance of Eel House engender fear; the weather is dangerous, even without the mysterious events; Hill creates tension and fear by the gradual build-up of frightening incidents; she uses the historical setting to evoke a tradition of ghost stories; fear is increased at the end because the story has apparently ended and the tragedy is unexpected.

17. *Oranges Are Not the Only Fruit*
The novel is semi-autobiographical and the narrative voice is that of a writer; the narrator is conscious of being the artist and her voice is intrusive; the Bible is dominant in her life and from the start she appreciates it as a literary text; her chapter titles are Books from the

Answers

Bible and relate stages in her development to those Books; this extract shows a precocious knowledge of art, music and poetry; she is aware of the quality of her creation and that she has more ability than others; her competitive nature and her self-belief drive her artistic and personal development; the inclusion of stories like those about Winnet show that she sees life as an artist does; her fate is to be a writer, not a missionary as she had thought, but the influences of her religious past are everywhere in her work.

Pages 56–57: Poetry

For questions 1–6, look at the mark scheme for Set A, Poetry on page 77. **[Maximum of [20]**

Depending on which poem you chose to compare, your answer might include some of the following points.

1. • Literal imagery: the poet describes the weather – 'Neutral Tones', 'When We Two Parted, 'Eden Rock', 'The Farmer's Bride'.
   • Pathetic fallacy as weather reflects mood – 'When We Two Parted', 'Neutral Tones', 'Porphyria's Lover'.
   • Pathetic fallacy in nature having human attributes ('gulping for breath') – 'Love's Philosophy'.
   • A real event remembered – 'Eden Rock', 'Walking Away', 'Mother, any distance', 'Before You Were Mine'.
   • Observing nature makes the poet consider his relationship – 'Love's Philosophy', 'Neutral Tones', 'Follower', 'Walking Away'.
   • Intensity of feeling expressed by imagery – Sonnet 29, 'Love's Philosophy', 'When We Two Parted'.
   • Literal imagery of the swans becomes extended metaphor for relationship – 'Neutral Tones'.
   • Form and structure – six three-line stanzas and a final two-line stanza, giving a sense of brief impressionistic memories – 'Eden Rock', 'Neutral Tones'.
   • Final short stanza brings a conclusion.

2. • Experience of a battle/war – 'The Charge of the Light Brigade', 'Exposure', 'Bayonet Charge'.
   • First person account of life-changing experience – 'The Prelude', 'Exposure'.
   • Poet adopts a persona – 'My Last Duchess'.
   • Poem based on reports/research not personal experience – 'The Charge of the Light Brigade', 'Bayonet Charge', 'War Photographer', contrast 'Exposure'.
   • Colloquial style conveying sense of conversation – 'Exposure'.
   • Individual haunted and shaped by memory – 'War Photographer', 'The Emigrée', 'The Prelude'.
   • Violent imagery and diction – 'Exposure', 'Bayonet Charge', 'War Photographer'.
   • The effect of war on individuals – 'Bayonet Charge', 'Poppies', 'War Photographer', 'Kamikaze'.
   • Use of present tense, showing how the past is still alive – 'Exposure', contrast 'Bayonet Charge', 'The Charge of the Light Brigade'.

• Structure – stanzas of equal length, varied line length followed by final one of two lines.
• No regular metre or rhyme scheme but some rhyme and half rhyme used – 'Exposure', 'Storm on the Island'.

3. • Use of a persona to tell the story of a relationship – 'La Belle Dame Sans Merci', 'A Child to his Sick Grandfather', 'The Manhunt'.
   • A relationship that is over – 'La Belle Dame Sans Merci', 'Neutral Tones', 'A Complaint', 'My Father Would Not Show Us'.
   • The speaker feels betrayed – 'La Belle Dame Sans Merci', 'Neutral Tones'.
   • The speaker has power over the Duchess – contrast with poems where the poet /persona is the victim – 'La Belle Dame Sans Merci', 'A Complaint', 'I wanna be yours', 'Valentine'.
   • Equal and unequal relationships and changing gender roles – 'Valentine', 'One Flesh', Sonnet 43.
   • Emphasis on the loved one's physical beauty – 'She Walks in Beauty', 'La Belle Dame Sans Merci', '1st Date – She, 1st Date – He'.
   • Regular metre (iambic pentameter) – Sonnet 43, and rhyming couplets – 'A Child to his Sick Grandfather'.
   • Single stanza narrative – 'Nettles'.

4. • Victims of war – 'The Man He Killed', 'Exposure', 'War Photographer', 'Poppies', 'The Destruction of Sennacherib', 'The Charge of the Light Brigade', 'Exposure', 'The Man He Killed', 'War Photographer'.
   • Victims in other situations – 'Half-Caste', 'No Problem', 'The Class Game', 'Cousin Kate', 'A Poison Tree', 'Exposure', 'Poppies'.
   • A sense of how life has changed after conflict – 'The Man He Killed', 'Cousin Kate'.
   • Victims are described by outside observers – 'War Photographer', 'The Destruction of Sennacherib', 'The Charge of the Light Brigade'.
   • Contrast sense of victimhood conveyed in first person – 'The Class Game', 'Half-Caste', 'Cousin Kate'.
   • Images of peaceful lives and nature used to evoke the past – 'Poppies', 'Exposure'.
   • Language and images of violence to describe destruction – 'War Photographer', 'The Destruction of Sennacherib'.
   • Unusual question and answer structure – compare playing with language/form in 'Belfast Confetti', 'No Problem', 'Half-Caste'.
   • Free verse – uneven lines, no rhyme – 'War Photographer', 'Poppies'.
   • Gentle, elegiac mood – 'Poppies', 'Exposure'.

5. • The beauty of the scene inspires the poet – 'To Autumn', 'Adlestrop', 'In Romney Marsh', 'Home Thoughts from Abroad'.
   • Contrasting view of London – 'London'.
   • Personal experience of a moment of reflection – 'Adlestrop', 'Where the Picnic Was', 'Nothing's Changed'.

- Contrast calm, positive mood with poet's feelings in 'Absence', 'Nothing's Changed', 'Stewart Island'.
- Sense of power and majesty – 'To Autumn', 'Stewart Island', 'First Flight'.
- Absence of detail about the poet and his life – 'Adlestrop', 'Home Thoughts from Abroad'. Contrast 'Where the Picnic Was', 'Absence', 'Stewart Island'.
- Petrachan (Italian) sonnet form. Regular forms also in 'In Romney Marsh', 'Adlestrop', 'Absence', 'London'.
- Personification of the city – 'To Autumn', 'In Romney Marsh'.
- Romantic poem – compare other poems by Romantics – 'To Autumn', 'London' – and consider influence on later poets.

6. **(a)**
- The poet addresses the loved one directly.
- The opening question leads to a series of answers.
- Repetition of 'I love thee'.
- Compares love to her love and grief for family and to religious faith.
- She sees love as eternal, lasting beyond death.
- Uses Petrachan (Italian) sonnet form, traditional form for love poetry.
- Use of caesura (broken lines) conveys her excitement and spontaneity, in contrast with regularity of form.

(b)
- Compare 'The Manhunt' – also a woman addressing a man, but here a persona, contemporary situation, different form and imagery.
- Compare 'Valentine', expressing love through imagery, contrasting comic tone.
- Compare 'Cozy Apologia', calmness of settled love, not passion of new love.

7. **(a)**
- Comparison of frost to a ghost sets mood and makes us think of death.
- Depressing mood continues with language like 'dregs', 'desolate' and 'weakening'.
- Landscape and weather reflects poet's mood – pathetic fallacy.
- In the second stanza Hardy places himself in the landscape.
- He associates the landscape with passing time, the century (19th) coming to an end.
- Uses an extended metaphor of a corpse, continuing morbid theme.
- Use of alliteration of hard 'c' gives a sharp, uncomfortable tone.
- There is a sudden change ('At once') with the sound of the thrush.
- Contrast of the 'joy' of the thrush with the death-like landscape.
- The age and weakness of the thrush makes his singing more extraordinary.
- Hardy sees the thrush as making an active choice to 'fling his soul'.
- The poet is unaware of the 'blessed Hope' but the thrush's song shows him the possibility of hope.
- Keats addresses the star.

- He directly compares himself to it; Hardy implicitly compares his mood and the thrush's.
- He describes how the star is 'steadfast' while saying he does not want to imitate it physically.
- He personifies the star, as Hardy personifies aspects of nature.
- He has a sense of wonder about nature and it inspires him rather than depressing him.
- His real subject turns out not to be the star but his love.
- It is a Petrachan (Italian) sonnet, the traditional form for a love poem. The octave focuses on the star and the sestet moves to his love.

(b)
- Other poems you might write about, focusing on how poets use natural imagery include 'Love and Friendship', 'The Sorrow of True Love', 'A Song', 'Fin de Fete', 'Morning Song'.

8. **(a)**
- Comparison of frost to a ghost sets mood and makes us think of death.
- Depressing mood continues with language like 'dregs', 'desolate' and 'weakening'.
- Landscape and weather reflects poet's mood – pathetic fallacy.
- In the second stanza Hardy places himself in the landscape.
- He associates the landscape with passing time, the century (19th) coming to an end.
- Uses an extended metaphor of a corpse, continuing morbid theme.
- Use of alliteration of hard 'c' gives a sharp, uncomfortable tone.
- There is a sudden change ('At once') with the sound of the thrush.
- Contrast of the 'joy' of the thrush with the death-like landscape.
- Religious imagery in 'evensong', 'soul' and 'carolings'.
- The age and weakness of the thrush makes his singing more extraordinary.
- Hardy sees the thrush as making an active choice to 'fling his soul'.
- The poet is unaware of the 'blessed Hope' but the thrush's song shows him the possibility of hope.
- Wordsworth's poem is also personal, about him in a landscape.
- Wordsworth's mood is also changed by nature.
- In this case the mood starts off light but darkens.
- Nature is personified.
- Nature is powerful and alive – there is a sense of it having a soul or spirit, as in Hardy's poem.
- The metre (iambic pentameter) is regular and steady.
- The poem is inward-looking, the poet analysing his feelings.
- While Hardy ends with a note of hope, Wordsworth is left disturbed and restless.

(b)

- Other poems you might write about, focusing on how the poets write about experiences which have a profound effect on the poet include 'The Man He Killed', 'Anthem for Doomed Youth', 'Punishment', 'There's a Certain Slant of Light', 'Vergissmeinnicht' and 'Partition'.

9. (a)

- Comparison of frost to a ghost sets mood and makes us think of death.
- Depressing mood continues with language like 'dregs', 'desolate' and 'weakening'.
- Landscape and weather reflects poet's mood – pathetic fallacy.
- In the second stanza Hardy places himself in the landscape.
- He associates the landscape with passing time, the century (19th) coming to an end.
- Uses an extended metaphor of a corpse, continuing morbid theme.
- Use of alliteration of hard 'c' gives a sharp, uncomfortable tone.
- There is a sudden change ('At once') with the sound of the thrush.
- Contrast of the 'joy' of the thrush with the death-like landscape.
- Religious imagery in 'evensong', 'soul' and 'carolings'.
- The age and weakness of the thrush makes his singing more extraordinary.
- Hardy sees the thrush as making an active choice to 'fling his soul'.
- The poet is unaware of the 'blessed Hope' but the thrush's song shows him the possibility of hope.
- Both poets write about themselves in a winter landscape.
- Sheers is not alone – he addresses the person ('you') he was with.
- He writes about the journey.
- The landscape suggests a melancholy mood.
- Reference to the mythical father and son, and the other person's age, suggest 'you' is his father.
- This is reinforced by the play on words in the title, 'Farther'.
- The father is almost part of the landscape: 'colour of the rocks'.
- They are fighting against the landscape and against time, as is Hardy.
- Sheers wants to preserve the moment in a photograph and in the poem.
- Like Hardy, he ends on a comparatively positive note – 'closer to you'.
- The poem is written in free verse, with irregular line lengths, no strong rhythm and no rhyme scheme – contrast 'The Darkling Thrush'.

(b)

- Other poems you might write about, focusing on place include, 'Cold Knap Lake', 'Midnight on the Great Western', 'The Bluebell', 'Holy Thursday' and 'Venus's-flytraps'.

Pages 58–59: Unseen Poetry

1. Look at the mark scheme for Set A, Unseen Poetry on page 79. **[Maximum of [20]**.

Your answer might include comments on:

(a) Comparison of frost to a ghost sets mood and makes us think of death; depressing mood continues with language like 'dregs', 'desolate' and 'weakening'; landscape and weather reflects poet's mood – pathetic fallacy; in the second stanza Hardy places himself in the landscape; he associates the landscape with passing time, the century (19th) coming to an end; uses an extended metaphor of a corpse, continuing morbid theme; use of alliteration of hard 'c' gives a sharp, uncomfortable tone; there is a sudden change ('At once') with the sound of the thrush; contrast of the 'joy' of the thrush with the death-like landscape; religious imagery in 'evensong', 'soul' and 'carolings'; the age and weakness of the thrush makes his singing more extraordinary; Hardy sees the thrush as making an active choice to 'fling his soul'; the poet is unaware of the 'blessed Hope' but the thrush's song shows him the possibility of hope.

(b) In both of them the poet is alone in the landscape; the landscape and weather are harsh in both, reflecting the poets' moods; in 'The Darkling Thrush' the poet's mood is changed but in 'Spellbound' it remains the same; Brontë does not say what the 'tyrant spell' is, whether it is from nature or her own feelings. Similarly Hardy does not explain his mood; Hardy writes about an incident in the past – Brontë writes in the present tense; Brontë's natural imagery is literal and simple, while Hardy uses an elaborate extended metaphor in the second stanza, as well as a simile in the first stanza; Brontë uses repetition and a refrain to give a sense of her situation; at first Brontë seems powerless but the last line suggests she is choosing to be where she is ('I will not'); while the weather depresses Hardy and his mood is rescued by the thrush, Brontë seems to rejoice in the 'dreary' night; both poems are regular in form and structure.